DESTINATION TOMBSTONE

ADVENTURES OF A PROSPECTOR

EDWARD SCHIEFFELIN
FOUNDER OF TOMBSTONE

Destination Tombstone: *Adventures of a Prospector*
Edward Schieffelin, Founder of Tombstone; Compiled by Marilyn F. Butler
Copyright ©1996 Marilyn F. Butler
    Publisher: Royal Spectrum Publishing, 2562 E. Evergreen, Mesa, AZ 85213, (602) 969-1591

Publisher's Cataloging-in-Publication

(prepared by Quality Books Inc.)

Schieffelin, Edward, 1847–1897.
    Destination Tombstone : adventures of a prospector / Edward Schieffelin.
    p. cm.
    Includes index.
    ISBN: 1-889473-98-7

    1. Schieffelin, Edward, 1847–1897. 2. Pioneers—Arizona—Tombstone—Biography. 3. Tombstone (Ariz.)—History. I. Title.

F819.T6S34 1996   979.1'53
                                                   QBI96-40203

Newspaper Articles: Excerpts from *San Francisco Chronicle*
Maps: Contributed by Mason Coggin, Director of Arizona
        Department of Mines and Mineral Resources
Photographs: Sonoran Desert, Grand Canyon and Edward Schieffelin's
        Tombstone on back cover by Luke Shane Wood
All Other Photographs: Family Archives
Editor: Jennifer Simmons
Book Design & Typesetting: SageBrush Publications, Tempe, Arizona
Cover Design: Running Changes, Phoenix, Arizona
Printing: Affiliated Lithographers, Phoenix, Arizona

DEDICATION

This book is dedicated to my mother, Eunice Musick, who never let me forget my family background; and to my husband, Glen Butler, who urged me to put this book together.

Marilyn Butler

ACKNOWLEDGMENTS

My special thanks to Dr. James McBride, Arizona State University, History Department; and Mason Coggin, Arizona Department of Mines and Minerals Resources, for their help and encouragement in publishing this book. I am very grateful for their faith and support.

TABLE OF CONTENTS

Edward Lawrence Schieffelin

Destination Tombstone

PROLOGUE

This manuscript is from the handwritten memoirs of Edward Lawrence Schieffelin, the discoverer of the Tombstone mines. They are first-hand tales of his adventures in prospecting through the West and Alaska.

From the time Ed was a small boy, all he ever wanted to do was be a prospector. These stories bring to life a determined man who dedicated himself to his obsession of finding a rich strike. Even after he found riches, he was not satisfied to stop and rest. He died fulfilling his lifelong dream of prospecting.

Edward Schieffelin personifies the typical prospector dedicated to unearthing a rich discovery of ore. His perseverance and drive led him to discover one of the most important silver mines in Western history. Without the discovery of the Tombstone mine, the town would not have existed. There would not have been the colorful events of the wild West. Millions of people have flocked to Tombstone to see the "OK Corral," "Boot Hill," and "The Town Too Tough to Die." Very few people know of Ed Schieffelin, its founder.

Ed's diaries give a first-hand account of his struggle and determination to search for the ultimate strike. His writings give an intimate image of his life and the role he plays in Western history. It richly shows the two driving forces in his life. The first being his early prospecting trips with the hardships and struggles and second, his never-ending drive to find ore. The prospecting trip to Alaska was a first-class adventure, since by that time he had the means to purchase the best and proper equipment.

His influence was felt throughout the West as well as the East where he went to sell stock in his mines. His lucky finds led other prospectors to follow in his footsteps and brought many people out to the Western states. The lure of silver and other precious ores led them to a region of the country that had previously been a little known territory, somewhere out in the wild West.

In the interest of how I obtained the original documents of Ed Schieffelin, they were passed down through the women of the family and kept in an old trunk. Ed's wife, Mary Elizabeth Brown Schieffelin, was my great grandmother.

As a small child, I remember hearing stories of "Uncle Ed," as he was known in our family. My grandmother, Josephine, was Ed's stepdaughter.

Ed met Mary Brown in Philadelphia, Pennsylvania. She was a widow and worked as an actress in the Philadelphia Traveling Theatrical Company. Mary's mother also worked there as the seamstress, making costumes. Mary had fallen on the wooden stage and gotten a splinter in her arm. The wound became infected, and as the theater company would not pay for her medical care, she went to an attorney to seek help for restitution for the medical bills. Mr. Schieffelin was visiting the same attorney. His attorney mentioned the plight of the lady in need, and Ed offered to pay her medical bills. Ed Schieffelin was a very generous man and was always willing to help anyone.

When Ed and Mary met they fell in love. Mary traveled with her mother and daughter to Colorado where she and Ed were married in La Junta in 1883. They settled in Alameda, California, where they had a large house on Central Avenue. In 1844, Ed and Mary moved to Los Angeles to be near his family. His father had died, having accidentally shot himself. In 1885, his brother, Albert, died of consumption.

Mary was living in Los Angeles when Ed was found dead in a cabin in Oregon where he had gone prospecting. In his will he requested that he be buried in the garb of a prospector with a pick and canteen, three miles west of

Mrs. Mary Schieffelin and her daughter, Josephine Brown

Tombstone, with a monument such as prospectors erect. Mary, along with Ed's mother and brother, Charles L. Schieffelin, went to Tombstone for the burial.

After Ed's death, Mary Schieffelin stayed in Los Angeles. In his will, Ed left her all his properties in Alameda and Santa Clara Counties. However, these properties were nonexistent at the time of his death. There was a suit pending in Philadelphia and Mary and Jay Schieffelin (Ed's brother) were to share the proceeds from that suit. She was also left $7,500 in cash and twelve University of Arizona bonds worth $1,000 each. Jay objected to Mary having the bonds. The will also indicated Mary was to have Ed's gold watch, gold scales,

RESIDENCE OF E.L. SCHIEFFELIN, CENTRAL AVE. ALAMEDA CAL.

Residence of Edward and Mary Schieffelin, Central Avenue, Alameda, California, 1884

assay furnace, revolver, rifle, valise, trunk of clothing, trunk of papers, three tin boxes of notebooks and papers. Only the papers used for this book remain in the family.

Mary Schieffelin accepted unsound financial advice, and the great fortune was gone by the time she died. As a result, in her later years when she became ill, it was necessary for her to go to the Los Angeles County Hospital, the irony being that Ed had donated the land where the hospital was built. Her doctor felt sorry for her and sent word to her daughter, Josephine Garrick, who lived in San Francisco. Josephine's husband, Walter, went down to Los Angeles and took Mary back to San Francisco where she lived until her death in 1918.

Mr. Schieffelin had given his rifle to a Mr. McDaniel of Phoenix, Arizona who was 15 years old at the time. Mr. McDaniel gave the rifle to his grandson, Cyrus Trask, who sold it in 1946.

The rifle was manufactured in 1860 at New Haven, Connecticut by the New Haven Arms Company. The repeating action of this rifle was one of the first ever manufactured. Patented by Mr. B. Tyler Henry, it used a .44 caliber, rim-fire metal cartridge. It had a magazine capacity for 15 cartridges. The rifle is now on display at the Schieffelin Hall in Tombstone, Arizona.

Also on display in Tombstone is a painting of Ed that had hung for many years in the California State Mining Bureau at the Ferry Building in San Francisco. In 1924, Ed's step-daughter, my grandmother, had it donated to the Arizona Pioneers Historical Society in Tucson, Arizona. It is presently on loan to Schieffelin Hall.

These historical papers are presented to add to the rich history of the "far West" and the territory of Arizona. It was through the efforts of men of vision as embodied in Edward Schieffelin that the territory of Arizona became noted by the United States and was brought into the Republic in 1912.

To give more clarity to the reader, I have taken the liberty of correcting some spelling and punctuation. However, I have kept Ed's usage of words and have spared correcting the translation to our twentieth-century language.

Marilyn F. Butler

SCHIEFFELIN FAMILY HISTORY

J ohann Jacob Schieffelin was born in Germany on December 10, 1702. The original name was spelled Schûffelin. He came to America for a visit, arriving in Philadelphia in 1743 on the ship *Ressonolli*. After returning to Germany, he came back to America with his family and settled in 1749. He died August 28, 1750.

His son, Jacob (2nd) was born in 1732. He married Regina Margaretha Kraften Ritschaurin in Philadelphia in 1756. They resided in Montreal, Canada, where Jacob died in 1769.

Jacob (3rd) was born in 1757. He and his wife, Hannah Laurence, resided in New York. They had four children. Jacob died in Manhattanville in 1835; his wife died in 1838.

Jacob (4th) was born in Montreal on April 20, 1793. He married Elizabeth Chapman and settled in New York. In 1825, Jacob took his family to Mexico City and later returned to New York where he founded a wholesale drug house which bore his name. After a few years of little profit, he moved the family to Tioga County, Pennsylvania where he extended his business to include agriculture.

Clinton Schieffelin was the oldest of Jacob's nine children. Clinton was born on February 16, 1823 in New York City. As a boy he worked on farms. He married Jane L. Walker who had come to America with her brother from Ireland. They lived in Tioga County, Pennsylvania. Clinton and his brother-in-law, Joe Walker, went to California in 1852 to try their luck in the gold fields. In 1853, he and Joe bought a land claim along the Rogue River in Oregon. Jane and her children crossed the plains and came West in 1857 to settle in Jackson County, Oregon. The Schieffelins had nine children. Laffette, born August 1, 1843, died April 8, 1844; Edward Lawrence, born October 8, 1847, died May 12, 1897; Albert Eugene, August 27, 1849-1885; Jane Elizabeth, September 2, 1851-October 5, 1931; Effingham, November 5, 1857-?; Charlotte, November 27, 1859-1895; Jacob, October 1, 1865-May 10, 1867; Theodore, October 6, 1867-September 17, 1881; Jay L., July 15, 1870-1934.

Clinton Schieffelin died April 15, 1884 from a gunshot wound. It has been questioned whether it was an accident or suicide. He and Jane lived in Los Angeles at the time. Albert died of consumption in 1885. He also lived in Los Angeles.

Jane Elizabeth (Lizzie) married Dr. Guiardo who gave up his medical practice and founded the first modern drug store in Los Angeles, California. Dr. Guiardo was the nephew of Pio Pico, the last of the Spanish governors of California.

In 1897, Edward was found dead in a lonely cabin about 20 miles from Canyonville, Oregon, where he had gone prospecting. The cause of death was described as a heart attack. In accordance with his will, he is buried in Tombstone, Arizona, under a monument such as prospectors build when locating a mining claim. His epitaph reads: "Ed Schieffelin, died May 12, 1897. Aged 49 years 8 months. A dutiful son, A faithful husband, A kind brother, A true friend."

Compiled by Marilyn F. Butler

Tombstone of Ed Schieffelin, near the town he founded–Tombstone. As he had requested, he was buried with a prospector's monument to mark his grave site.

Destination Tombstone

INTRODUCTION

What makes the memoirs of Edward Schieffelin so unusual, and valuable, is his experiences transcend, both regionally and temporally, the mining rushes of the American West. Schieffelin's experiences range from the Rogue River area of Oregon in the 1860s, through Nevada, Utah, and Arizona in the 1870s, and culminate in an extremely well-equipped expedition up the Alaskan Yukon River in the 1880s. In these accounts of those times and places, he displays a remarkable memory, a flair for description, both of people and events, and a forthrightness and honesty that is truly refreshing.

Edward Schieffelin was born on the family farm in Pennsylvania in 1847. Soon after his father left to head west to the gold camps of California. By the time Ed was 9 years old, the family had settled on a farm in Oregon. The first of these memoirs tells of Ed at the age of 19 leaving the farm to head to the mining camps along the Rogue River. Mining in Oregon was primarily river mining and required a great deal of work diverting water into long toms, sluices and crude hydraulic systems. His account of this trip describes the struggles, as well as the naiveté, of a young miner, and reads almost like an account from Mark Twain's *Roughing It*.

By the 1870s, the focus for mining had shifted east to the Great Basin and a different type of mining. Nevada was silver country. While much of the history of mining in Nevada centered on the Comstock Lode and the western side of the state, there was mining activity in the other areas of Nevada also. Miners from California and the coastal camps of Oregon and Washington flowed into the region. From 1870 to 1873, Pioche, Nevada, in the southeastern part of the state, was booming, and Schieffelin joined the surge of prospectors.

Most of the mining development of Nevada involved silver lode, a mineral technique beyond the knowledge and ability at that time of the average American prospector. It is possible that Schieffelin's later knowledge of and interest in silver mining came from this period of his life.

During the spring of 1872, he explored much of southeastern Nevada, southwestern Utah and northwestern Arizona. However, constantly on the move during this period, his activities centered in the isolated region where Nevada, Utah, and Arizona come together north of the Grand Canyon. Ed relates several incidents that reveal a great deal of the hazards and fears of the lonely prospector. Within a few brief weeks, he encountered marauding Indians, escaped from a flash flood in a narrow canyon and met a Mormon who provided a chilling and obviously biased account of the Mountain Meadows Massacre.

Also, the 1870s were years of dynamic growth for Arizona mining. Major discoveries were made with some of the most vigorous activity occurring in the southeastern part of the territory. Although the Arizona Territory was abandoned by the United States military at the beginning of the Civil War, the Bascom Affair and the killing of Mangos Colorados by Apaches led by Cochise, brought military attention to the region again. President Grant sent agents to establish reservations for the Apaches, and the Army transferred Colonel George Crook to the territory to prepare a military campaign against those who refused to be contained. In December of 1872, using small, self-sustaining units equipped with pack mules and guided by Indian scouts, the Army soon drove most of the Apaches onto the reservations. Often when these patrols went out from Fort Huachuca, Ed Schieffelin went along with them for protection and companionship.

Since 1857, the mineral potential of the area east of Fort Huachuca had been well-known. During that year, Frederick

Brunckow, employed by the Sonora Exploring and Mining Company, had staked a claim in the San Pedro Mountains of the Sonora Valley. In 1859, Brunckow organized the St. Louis Mining Company and began working the claim. Striking a rich silver vein, he and his partners hired Mexican workers and mined the claim until June 1860 when the laborers attacked and killed all of the company's employees, including Brunckow. Afterwards, the mine changed ownership several times, although each owner only performed the necessary annual assessment work to keep title to the claim. Brunckow was right about the Sonora Valley being a "vast mineral treasure." By March of 1877, Ed Schieffelin was prospecting in the southeastern part of the Arizona Territory. After years of persistence, his efforts eventually paid off by finding a rich silver vein within working distance of the Brunckow Mine.

In these memoirs, Ed Schieffelin describes having very little money. He, therefore, tried to secure a grubstake from several Tucson merchants. However, all efforts failed and his only hope for help was to find his brother, Al Schieffelin. In a forthright description of his physical and financial condition when he arrived at the Signal Mine in southern Mojave County where Al was working, Ed reports he had only one dollar left in his pocket. After convincing Al and Richard Gird to assay ore samples from the Brunckow Mine, Ed and they left Mojave County for the riches of Tombstone. With money that Richard Gird put up for a grubstake, the three began working from the Brunckow Mine site. They soon discovered the rich vein of silver and named their first mines the Lucky Cuss and the Toughnut deposits. In 1878, they formed the Tombstone Mining District, which set in motion one of the most spectacular mining rushes in Arizona and American history.

A town site was selected by a Tucson merchant named John B. (Pie) Allen, and was named Tombstone after Ed

Schieffelin's first claim. Following a period of conflicting efforts to lay out and incorporate the small community, in December of 1879, the citizens finally received approval from the Pima County Board of Incorporation. Despite this contentious start, Tombstone grew rapidly, and by mid-1881 boosters were boasting of a population of between 7,000 and 10,000, plus claiming it was the most important city in Arizona territory. By the time Tombstone was considered a town, Ed and Al had sold their interest in the mines and each received $600,000 for their shares. Richard Gird sold out a year later and received a greater profit.

In 1882, Ed Schieffelin was a rich man, but he was still a prospector. Studying maps of the Western hemisphere had convinced him that there was a mineral belt running southward through the continent to the Arctic. Accordingly, in the spring of 1883, he built a boat to his specifications, hand picked a crew and sailed up the Yukon River in search of gold. While he found traces of gold, he did not find enough to make mining profitable. After returning to the United States he married Mary Elizabeth Brown, and they settled in Alameda, California. On occasion Ed continued to prospect, and on a trip in 1897 he died in Oregon. As he had requested, his family returned his body to Arizona and buried him on a small knoll north of Tombstone, the town he brought into existence.

In conclusion, the recollections of Edward Schieffelin provide a view of mining in a variety of areas over a period of sixteen years. He describes the work, fear, terror, awe of nature and natives, guilt and deceit, as well as honesty and fair-play of the prospector. Although his memoirs were written long after the events, his recollections of people and places remained sharp and perceptive, giving us a vivid description of life throughout the mining frontier of the Old West.

Dr. James McBride

With a pick in one hand, and a rifle in the other, Ed Schieffelin was a prospector's prospector.

I well remember my first prospecting trip.
I guess I was about seventeen. It wasn't
my first prospecting by any means.
but the first time. I packed a horse
and went out into the mountains.
to be gone any length of time. and
then it was only for a couple of weeks
and only about ten miles. from home,
but at that time I thought it was a
long ways. until I got to wondering
how those that went through the
country first must have managed.
and probably what they thought when
they was hundreds of miles from
any body and Indians everywhere.
then "it didn't seem so far nor as
much of a trip as it did the first
night or two. The first night. the
old work horse. that belonged to
Father, that I had pressed into service
to pack my out fit. got loose. by a
coyote cutting the rope. and went back
home. leaving me entirely alone.
my first impulse was to go after
him. but on thinking over the matter
a while. concluded as I was where
I wanted to be. and no immediate
use for him. and that iff I got

CHAPTER 1

BATTLE GROUND

I well remember my first prospecting trip. I guess I was
about seventeen. It wasn't my first prospecting by any
means, but the first time I packed a horse and went out into
the mountains to be gone any length of time. And then it
was only for a couple of weeks and only about ten miles from
home. But at that time I thought it was a long ways until I
got to wondering how those that went through the country
first must have managed and probably what they thought
when they was hundreds of miles from anybody and Indians
every where. Then it didn't seem so far nor as much of a trip
as it did the first night or two. The first night the old work
horse that belonged to Father that I had pressed into service
to pack my outfit got loose by a coyote cutting the rope and
went back home leaving me entirely alone. My first impulse
was to go after him. But on thinking over the matter awhile,
concluded as I was where I wanted to be and no immediate
use for him, and that if I got him again the same thing would
most likely occur. So that I would let him go until I wanted

to either go home or somewhere else then go and get him. For I was sure that he had gone straight home which I afterwards found to be so. I guess I had been there about a week, sinking holes in gulches and creeks and gouging around one place and another. Occasionally finding a little gold but nothing of any consequence. When one evening about dusk, I went along up the main creek on which I was camped to see if I couldn't kill a deer. But it was too late so I didn't go far but came back to camp as I went without any deer.

Just up on the side of the mountain, a couple of hundred yards or so was quite a thicket in the head of a small gulch that ran down close to where I was camped. I was just · starting a fire to get supper, having set my rifle, an old muzzle loader, against a big pine tree within a few feet of where I was building a fire, when all at once the damnedest racket I ever heard started right up in the thicket spoken of. For a second or two I didn't realize what it was and went for my rifle and my hat fell off. Whether I knocked it off in my haste to get my rifle, or whether my hair raising on end pushed it off, to this day I don't know. But I do know I was very badly scared for a little while. In fact until the fight ended, which it did in a very few minutes, and I heard them run it was too dark to see. But I heard them run over the point away from where I was, which was a great relief to me. For it wasn't long after the fight began before I was satisfied that it was a couple of Grizzlies fighting. Although I had never heard bear fighting before, but from the noise, which sounded to me worse than if all the dogs in the country was fighting at the same time, with an occasional clap of thunder thrown in, I was sure it was bear.

There was plenty of them there I knew. Although I had not seen any. Still I saw their tracks every day and panther as well, who I would hear scream almost every night. And would sometimes think sure it was a woman's voice so much so that once or twice I answered, but receiving no reply, knew it was a panther.

In the morning, I went up to have a look at the battle ground, but I didn't find no dead bear. As I had read about that usually where wild animals that way got a fighting, one of them got killed. It wasn't so in this case. Nor was there blood, flesh, nor any bones. Only here and there a little tuft of fur. But the brush looked as if a tornado had struck it, and the ground was some what scratched where they had struck their claws in. Otherwise, one would never know there had been a bear in the country. But the noise they make, especially where there is heavy timber and at night, makes up for all else. At least a boy, that being his first experience, will think so.

I expected to meet with some of them while I was there, but I didn't, and I was there some time after that. Long enough to satisfy myself that there was no mines there, nor has there been any found yet.

Along about 66. during my first experiences
of Prospecting in the placer mines of South
western Oregon. In a small Gulch that
empties into a small creek called Birdseye
Creek. not far from Louse Creek. I thought
I had found rich diggings. and according
-ly built me a cabin. dug a ditch nearly
two miles in length. and made prepara
-tions generaly for a winters work. but
all for nothing. for I did not make a qua
-rter of a dollar out of it.

One evening. after being all ready to go too
work. but having no water, for the rains
that winter was late in coming. I had
been hunting and was coming home.
when not far from the cabin I saw a
smoke, which at first sight I took too
be the cabin a fire. but which proved to
be couple of men, from another mining
camp about twelve miles from there.
who had came on the creek that day a
Prospecting. And seeing that somebody
lived at in the cabin, and would most
likely be there at night. concluded to
camp there. so as too interview him
that evening. and learn what they
could concerning the prospects on the
creek for diggings. And when I go

CHAPTER 2

SWAPPED LIES

Along about '66, during my first experience of prospecting in the placer mines of southwestern Oregon in a small gulch that empties into a small creek called Birdseye Creek, not far from Rogue River, I thought I had found rich diggings and accordingly built me a cabin. Dug a ditch nearly two miles in length and made preparations generally for a winter's work. But all for nothing for I didn't make a quarter of a dollar out of it.

One evening after being all ready to go to work, but having no water, for the rains that winter was late in coming, I had been hunting and was coming home. When not far from the cabin, I saw a smoke which at first sight I took to be the cabin afire. But which proved to be couple of men from another mining camp about twelve miles from there who had come on the creek that day a prospecting. And seeing that somebody lived in the cabin and would most likely be there at night, concluded to camp there so as to interview him that evening and learn what they could concerning the prospects on the creek for diggings. And when I got there I took them into the cabin. Although they could have went in theirselves for there was no lock to the door. And as they had some grub with them, I didn't give them any supper but did their breakfasts.

During the evening, we told stories, swapped lies and made it pass very pleasantly. And I also learned that they had got there early in the day, about the middle of the forenoon and had been up and down the creek occasionally washing a pan of dirt. But they had found nothing encouraging and one of them who owned what tools (a pan) that they had brought with them, said that in the morning he was going back home as he didn't like the creek and didn't believe there was anything of any account on it.

The other one seemed to want to stay a few days as I had told them that they could stay there with me and I had plenty of provisions and they their own blankets. There was nothing to hinder them from staying as long as they liked. But Shoe Butcher, which I afterwards learned was his name, getting it from mending boots, wouldn't stay. And the next morning bright and early, struck out for home. So I told Palmer, the other fellow, an Englishman, that if he wanted to try the creek farther that I would loan him a pick, shovel and pan and that he could stay there in the cabin with me. That there was plenty of grub, all he would have to do was cook it when I was away, which I would be during the day for a few days. For I was going to help George Burns finish a ditch that he was digging and who lived on the left hand fork of the creek some three miles above, but that I would be there nights. And for all of which he seemed to be very thankful.

So I got the pick, pan and shovel for him, took my rifle and started for Burns'. And he shouldered his tools and said that he would go along up with me and see Burns' diggings and then prospect from there down to the forks and up the

right hand fork, as he had been on it the day before and saw
a place that looked well. Which was all right and when we
got up to Burns', after looking at the claim, he went up on
the ditch with us and after standing around awhile, went
away and after he had gone, George says to me, "That fellow
won't do any prospecting." "Why?" I says. "Oh, he is no
prospector. He ain't shaped right."

That night or evening rather, when going down the trail,
I thought I could see his tracks all the way down but thought
nothing of it particular. Only it was a queer way of
prospecting, to follow a trail all the time. But when I got to
the cabin, I found out that he had done no prospecting for
there set the tools up by the side of the door, perfectly clean
as I had given him in the morning. And had went in, cooked
his dinner and I suppose eat it. It was gone at all events, and
so was he. And the interior of that cabin looked like the devil
for he had been through and turned every thing topsy turvy
looking for something. What it was I don't know unless
money. I looked all around but could miss nothing whatever.
Everything was there only scattered around.

When it, I suppose, was a couple of months afterwards
that my brother, Al, came up one day and was looking at
some quartz that I had brought in from time to time when
out hunting or traveling around and would see a nice piece,
bring it in and throw it down by the side of the door. And
had accumulated quite a little pile and thought he saw some
fine gold in one of the pieces and went to get a very fine
magnifying or quartz glass that had been given me a year or
two previous and which I had always kept in a little box
nailed up to one of the logs over the head of my bed, which
served as a shelf to set a candle on at night when I wanted to
lay and read as well as a shelf for such small things. But the
glass was gone and calling to me that the glass was gone, or
that I had changed it, but I hadn't for I had not used it. I

didn't know when and we both hunted high and low. Looked every where and hated to give up the search, when we found it was useless, because it was a very powerful fine glass. One that I not only valued for its quality but as a gift. At last it dawned on me that that fellow, Palmer, had taken it. Not being able to find anything else that was handy to carry and would be of any use to him and seeing it was an extra fine glass, had taken it, feeling sure that it would be sometime before I missed it unless by accident. It was a mean trick and as Burns had said, he wasn't shaped right for a prospector. But he was gone and so was the glass, and I never saw or heard of him afterwards.

In March 72, after spending the winter in Cave
Valley, Nev. about seventy miles north of Pioche.
cutting picketts, to make a grub stake. for the
summers prospecting, I started for the Gran
Canon of the Colorado. and on my way
down, about thirty miles below Pioche I
over took a young mormon, who was
going to Pioche St George Souther Utah
it being on my road. we traveled toget
-her the ballance of the way. a couple of
days or so. and on our journey passed
the Mountain Meadows. made famous
by that dark and bloody deed perpetr
ated by the mormons, I think in 58.
And my companion; being a mormon
born and raised amongst them, knew
pretty well their ways. although at
that time. he had began to realize their
evil ways. and was begining to be an
apostate. And as we rode along through
the little green Meadows of the Moun
tains he told me the story of their the
massacre of the emigrants a few
years previous. and which was still
fresh in the minds of the people of
the world,
He began by pointing out the spot. show
him. as well as the story told. by one of

CHAPTER 3

POOR HELPLESS CREATURES

In March '72, after spending the winter in Cave Valley, Nev., over about twenty miles north of Pioche, cutting pickets to make a grub stake for the summer's prospecting, I started for the Grave Canyon of the Colorado and on my way down about thirty miles below Pioche, I overtook a young Mormon who was going to St. George, Southern Utah. It being on my road, we traveled together the balance of the way. A couple of days or so and on our journey passed the Mountain Meadows made famous by that dark and bloody deed perpetuated by the Mormons. I think in (18)58. And my companion, being a Mormon born and raised amongst them, knew pretty well their ways. Although at that time he had began to realize their evil ways and was beginning to be an apostate. And as we rode along through the little green meadows of the mountains, he told me the story of the

massacre of the emigrants a few years previous and which
was still fresh in the minds of the people of the world.

He began by pointing out the spot shown him as well as
the story told by one of the participants, but who long since
had repented and was sorry that he had ever had a hand in
it. Where they camped was on a very pretty grassy slope
about half a mile from where the battle occurred at the head
of the canyon and where the doomed little band, entrenched
by breast works thrown up under their wagons, fought their
worse than heartless foe all day.

When late in the afternoon as the sun was sinking
behind the distant mountains, bordering the beautiful valley
of the Los Angeles, where they was going to make their homes,
the Mormons finding that they was unable to dislodge them
without great loss to themselves, concluded to try the means
of false friendship and thereby gain possession of their
arms when they ceased firing and all became still, like the
calm before a storm. And John D. Lee, the leader of that
treacherous and wicked band and the only one among the
many participants that was ever tried, condemned and
executed, for one of the darkest deeds that was ever recorded
in the annuals of religious history, promised those poor half
famished creatures, far from friends, surrounded by enemies
of the worst type, that if they would give up their arms that
he would take them safely back to Cedar City about half
way back to Salt Lake.

The emigrants, after consulting, being out of water,
surrounded by armed, what they thought hostile Indians, and
some lay in the cold embrace of death, others wounded, they
concluded to accept those kindly offers by supposed friends,
not knowing or thinking for a moment that it was Mormons
disguised as Indians, as well as Indians themselves, that they
had been fighting all day, and which sent them all but two
little girls to their graves.

For as soon as the Mormons got possession of their arms, they marched them, men, women, children, one and all along before them up to where they had camped the night before. When, from a signal given by the leader, the slaughter commenced. Mormons and Indians vying with each other for the palm of cruelty. Sparing none but the two little girls who afterwards were put to death in Salt Lake City because they recognized one of their mother's dresses on one of the women in the family who they was living with.

The Mormons were tenfold worse than the Indians and committed acts of licentious barbarism, unprecedented even in the imaginations of the Novelists. For not only did they tear infants from the breasts of weeping Mothers, and by the heels dash their brains out, the blood and brains bespattering the garments of the swooning Mother as she fell to the ground. But amidst that awful scene, some crying for mercy, Mothers shrieking for dead children clasped to their breasts, groans of the wounded, the death rattle of the dying, the religious curses of the Mormons and that ever blood curdling yell amid suffering, that was whoop of the hostile Indians. And by the dead body of the Father and under the staring gaze of the expiring Mother, those incarnate fiends of human shape ravished young girls. Some not yet in their teens and when not unconscious, some would hold their struggling victim while others, as many as desired, accomplished their purpose. Then in the name of God end the sufferings of the poor helpless creatures by cutting their throats. Then leaving the mutilated and exposed bodies for wild beasts and disgusting vultures to prey upon. They gathered the stock and turned it over to the church while the plunder they divided among themselves. And he said that at that time, that he knew a family that had one of the pianos and made their boasts that it was taken from that train and the fate of the two little girls tells where the clothes of the party went.

The Mormons claim that it was done for revenge, but it was done for plunder for it was the richest train that ever crossed the plains. The stock was all thoroughbred and at that time could readily be distinguished from their more inferior kind whenever met.

It is hard to believe that such atrocious crimes could be committed by civilized human beings, by men who were fathers, husbands with daughters of their own, brothers of innocent sisters, and sons of loving mothers, but to those that has had experiences among the Mormons and knows the abject submission that ignorance and religion reduces mankind and their fanatic hatred for Gentiles or anybody antagonistic to any of their religious teachings and the influence that the church has over them. And that church ruled by a licentious avaricious revengeful man who is a vain absolute despot in whose breast, like the Kings of bygone ages, no spark of suffering humanity ever caused it one single pang of remorse, can readily see that there is no crime too horrible for them to commit. Is it any wonder that crimes so revolting to more sensitive natures as to cause them to shed tears of pity for the victims and turn from the perpetrators with a loathing and disgust beyond description are committed with an indifference and an abandonment of feeling that is perfectly indescribable. And whenever the dark mantle that enshrouds Utah is thrown off and she stands to the world in her true light, there will be revealed innumerable dark crimes and suffering that has been hoarse, that will be beyond the power of tongue or pen to describe.

Editor's Note: This is an accurate transcription of Schieffelin's writings, however, others tell a different account of this event.

If you want to get real badly scared,
just get caught in a box canon once
during one of those thunder storms
or cloud bursts, as they are usualy
called in Nevada and Arizona.
Once will do you, and you always
afterwards will take good care
to be out of them, whenever
there is one of those storms com
-ing up

For too be riding down one of
those box canons, so thick along
the Colorado River in some places
and no immediate place in which
to get out, the walls on either side
hundreds of feet high, and hear
that roar, that you ever afterwards
recolect, and wont mistake it
either, coming along, getting
nearer, and nearer, and you have
no idea how much farther you
will have to go, before there is
a break in the walls so that you
can get out, and wait for it too
pass, which only takes a few min
-utes, It dont seem to travel fast
but you undertake to get away
from one once, and you will
think that it travels with

CHAPTER 4

LOOKING BACK OVER YOUR SHOULDER

If you want to get real badly scared, just get caught in a box canyon once during one of those thunderstorms or cloud bursts, as they are usually called in Nevada and Arizona. Once will do you, and you always afterward will take good care to be out of them whenever there is one of those storms coming up.

For to be riding down one of those box canyons so thick along the Colorado River in some places and no immediate place in which to get out, the walls on either side hundreds of feet high and hear that roar that you ever afterwards recollect and won't mistake it either, coming along getting nearer and nearer and you have no idea how much further you will have to go before there is a break in the walls so that you can get out and wait for it to pass, which only takes a few minutes. It don't seem to travel fast but you undertake to get away from one once, and you will think that it travels with the speed of lightening. And after they say that under very dangerous circumstances all the mean things a man ever done in his life, in fact his whole life comes up before him. But I don't think you would have time to think much about your meanness when going down a canyon on the run with your pack mule with her head up and two or three jumps ahead of you, and you every jump digging the spurs in to the flanks of your horse trying to make him increase his jumps. And looking back over your shoulder, see that roll of water, mud, logs, sticks and rocks making a wall six or eight feet high, tumbling and rolling, sweeping all before it, and knowing that at least half a mile had to be made over the rocks, cactus, brush and such things without any road before you would have a chance to escape, you would think of anything but that desired place. And until you was out on the side looking at it sweep by, that you would know that you ever lived before.

In the spring of 72. I had about as close a
call as I ever had, in the Virgin Canon, about
sixty miles from St George. just below
where the Beaver dam Wash empties into
the virgin River.

As usual I was alone. and the nearest
white men to me was St George that
I had left the day before. And iff they had
have known what I was, would have been
glad had I met the fate that at first
seemed there was no escape from. and
afterwards look more miraculous to me.
than at the time. Before I got to St
George, on my road a young mormon
over took me. and we traveled together
for three or four days. And he warned
me to do no prospecting in that country
at that time. For he said, you no doubt
have heard, which I had, of parties com
-ing down here into the Buckskin Moun
-tains. and never being heard off. the
mormons could tell what had become
of them iff they was a mind too, as you
go on about your bussiness. nobody here
would suspect you of being a Prospector
but would take you for some cattle deal
er, from some of the mining camps up
in Nevada. down here looking for beef

CHAPTER 5

ONE MAN ALONE

In the spring of '72, I had about as close a call as I ever had in the Virgin Canyon about sixty miles from St. George, just below where the Beaver Dam Wash empties into the Virgin River.

As usual I was alone and the nearest white man to me was in St. George that I had left the day before. And if they had have known what I was, would have been glad had I met the fate that at first seemed there was no escape from. And afterwards, look more miraculous to me than at the time. Before I got to St. George, on my road, a young Mormon overtook me, and we traveled together for three or four days. And he warned me to do no prospecting in that country at that time. For he said, "You no doubt have heard," which I had, "Of parties coming down here into the Buckskin Mountains and never being heard of. The Mormons could tell what had become of them if they was a mind to. So you go on about your business. Nobody here would suspect you of being a prospector, but would take you for some cattle

dealer from some of the mining camps up in Nevada down
here looking for beef. And if you keep your mouth shut
they won't know the difference, and there are lots of those
Mountain Meadows massacre fellows in here one place and
another. I could show several of them as we go into and in
St. George. I was born and raised a Mormon, but that don't
make me one at heart. And did they know my mind in
regard to them, although my parents are good Mormons, my
chances would be slim. You folks think you know something
of them, but you don't. So you take my advice, one who
knows, and don't you do any prospecting nor talk about it
while you are in the vicinity." Which I did to the letter, and
no doubt you think by this time that my adventure was with
the Mormons having said so much about them. But it
wasn't. It was with the Indians. And I mention them and
what my companion told me so that you may know what I
mean when I say having traveled through the Mormons all
right and getting where I thought I was beginning to be
safe, met up with what I am now going to tell you in a very
few words.

As I have already mentioned, it was in the Virgin
Canyon close to the Beaver Dam Wash. I had traveled all
day without seeing any signs of Indians and would not have
paid much attention to them if I had, for those Indians had
for a few years previous been considered peaceful, and I had
heard of their committing no depredations. It was a little before
one of those beautiful sunsets that is seen no other place in
the world but on those deserts of those southern countries,
but which I am not going to try and describe. The road all
the afternoon had been running over a high mesa which
virtually made the Virgin Canyon and coming into the
Beaver Dam Wash, followed it down into the canyon. And
for some distance the river as well as one side of the Canyon
is very crooked and thickly studded with willows. So that an

army of men might be in some of those nooks in the side of the Canyon and on the opposite side of the river from where the road runs and not be seen.

And so it proved with me for I had just entered the canyon and crossed the river when through an opening in the willows I saw a lot of Indians who had apparently just got there and made camp, not having made any fire yet. Nor was they on the look out for anybody on such an unfrequented road as that one was, especially one man alone. And probably the only one in six months before. So that we both saw one another at the same time. He fetched a whoop which in that canyon sounded like thunder, and about sixty of them, all armed with guns, started for me. Some to get behind me and come ahead to keep me from making a dash for it. And long before I could have got where they filed across the road ahead of me, had I tried. They was there and coming to meet me in a slow trot. And there was no use to undertake to go back for all they had to do was to climb over a point that divided the Wash from the canyon and not over two hundred yards across to get to the road on that side, and I would have to ride a half a mile or so.

So my only way was to put a bold front on and trust to strategy for there was too many to fight. Besides I hadn't seen them all for I could still see some standing in camp and hear a great many holler. And when they closed in around me, leaving a circle of about forty feet across for me to perambulate in, which considering the circumstances, my Mustang almost beside herself with fright and was plunging, bucking and shying all at once and the same time, which kept me very busy to keep my seat, and I believe is what saved me. For she drew their attention and I supposed amused them, and before they knew what I was about, I yelled to them to *vamoose* (a Spanish word meaning go), wave my hand for them to stand aside and put spurs deep into her flanks causing her to act like one mad. I made a break through the circle nearly riding one of them down before he could crowd himself into the crowd that was falling back to get out of our way. And away we went down that canyon like the wind. Expecting any minute until we was out of range and sight to hear a gun go off and a bullet whistling if not feel it. Nor did we stop until I was sure that I was out of all danger as far as they were concerned. And I rode until late in the night but not fast of course. Then rode off the road and camped without unsaddling with the end of the stake rope tied to my arm so that in case I fell asleep, which I didn't, she could not break loose from me in case any of them undertook to follow me.

And starting again before daybreak the next morning, I arrived at St. Thomas, Nevada, where the Muddy and Virgin Rivers come together, about two o'clock in the afternoon. All safe and sound. The second day after my arrival, some parties on their way to Arizona, coming down the Meadow Valley Wash until it empties into the Muddy, then down that to St. Thomas and on to Arizona, found where three men who had left Pioche a few days before them, well armed and equipped with plenty of ammunition, had been killed by the Indians, about forty or fifty miles from St. Thomas in the Meadow Valley Wash at a place called Indian Spring. And was supposed to have been done the third morning previous, making it the morning of the same on which I was surrounded in the afternoon and the two places were only about forty miles apart across the country the way Indians generally travel. And taking all the circumstances in consideration, that being the way they would naturally go to get to the Buckskin Mountains, their place of refuge, I am certain they are the same Indians that on that morning had killed the three men at Indian Spring in the Meadow Valley Wash. For their actions at the time was entirely different from friendly Indians. And that was what scared me and made me run for it. For if they had acted as they ought, had they meant no mischief, I should have stopped, got down out of the saddle and had a talk with them, but the moment I saw them move, I knew something was wrong and what ever kept them from firing on me before I had gone a hundred yards, is more than I can tell.

About the hardest ride I ever had. was in
the summer of. 72 in Arizona. from. old Fort
Rock, on the california road, by way of Hardy-
ville. to Camp Walaipai. The Apaches
those days was. all over the Territory.
and it was dangerous to be safe any
place. But the Prescot country was considered the worst off. all. which was
probaly twenty five miles. farther on
from Camp Walaipai. And before getting
to Camp Walaipai. the road passed over
Juniper Mountain. and down Juniper
Canion. A very bad place for Indians.
and horse men. or parties of but a few men
always traveled it in the night. it being
much safer. because they couldn't see you
any distance.

At the time I speak off. the Walaipai
Indians. who for a short time, had been
on peacable terms with the Whites. was
in that section of the country hunting
and their fires. at night could be seen
in all directions, On going from Beal
Springs to Fort Rock. I took Chances. and
rode it in the day time. and during
the day. saw lots of Walaipai's. but
paid no paticular attention. any more
than to occasionaly stop and pass a few
words. with them. as I usualy done

me that there was some narrow places in it where a man on the side of the road could stick a butcher knife in a fellow as he passed. For some places the banks over hung the road and covered with thick brush. But I didn't know how the road run and the way I had to go might be in a circle while an Indian could cut across, get there ahead and wait for me to come up. And that was a signal of some kind. There was no mistaking. And you bet I let out in earnest and if ever man rode for his life, I did. Nor did I slacken speed when I got to Juniper Canyon and how I (I have been over the road since in daylight) got through that canyon without my horse falling, has ever since been a mystery. For it is not only steep but at that time the road was full of large boulders and holes washed out by recent rains. But we went down a flying, nor did the horse require any urging. And came out all right at an old fellow's by the name of Brewster's about a half a mile from Camp Walaipai at two clock in the morning having ridden that fifty miles over a rough strange road in five hours on a Mustang that was worth about thirty dollars. Nor to all appearances was she any the worse for the ride next morning.

About the hardest trip I ever took, was
in the spring of 72. when I with
four others went up in the Grandest
of all canon. the Grand Canon of
the Colorado River. Although it
was short less than a mouth
it was a hard one.

It was a long in the latter part
of March, that there was about
two hundred of us left St Thomas
on the Muddy. in the southeast
corner of Nevada, with two boats
loaded, already for launching
except carting and pitching, on
wagons, for the Canon. about forty
miles a cross the country. There
was two parties with boats, four
in ours. and six in the other.
The rest, when we got too the river.
we was going to ferry their out
fits a cross, swim their horses.
go a cross the country until they
struck Diamond River. folow it
down, and see iff they couldn't
get into the Grand Canon that
way. Our party from some
cause or other was delayed one
day at the Muddy. which off
course threw us behind in

CHAPTER 7

THE
GRANDEST
OF ALL
CANYONS

About the hardest trip I ever took was in the spring of '72 when I, with four others, went up in the Grandest of all canyons, the Grand Canyon of the Colorado River. Although it was short, less than a month, it was a hard one.

It was along in the latter part of March that there was about two hundred of us left St. Thomas on the Muddy, in the southeast corner of Nevada, with two boats loaded, all ready for launching, except caulking and pitching, on wagons, for the Canyon about forty miles across the country. There was two parties with boats. Four in ours and six in the other. The rest, when we got to the river we was going to ferry their outfits across, swim their horses, go across the country until they struck Diamond River, follow it down, and see if they couldn't get into the Grand Canyon that way. Our party, from some cause or other, was delayed one day at the Muddy, which of course threw us behind in getting to the river. And when we got there, the boys with the other boat, some was fishing and some setting around the camp fire, and left only one man (Bush Dulin) to work at the boat. The others with horses was a couple or so miles above, close to the mouth of the Canyon. Us fellows with boats, on account of the wagons, had to follow a big wash down and which emptied into the river at that place. The only place where we, in that neighborhood, could get to the river.

At this time there was a party up in the canyon with a boat prospecting and had been for some time, called Cook's party. And everybody was excited and speculating on what they had probably found. Some would gamble that they had found rich diggings or they wouldn't stay so long. And that if there was rich diggings anywheres in that Canyon they would find it or keep going until they got to the Marble Canyon, something like two hundred miles up the Grand Canyon, until they got to the river when their feathers fell and acted as if they was sorry that they had started and was sitting around as above described as if waiting for something to turn up, so as to have an excuse to turn back. And there was nothing there to scare anybody only it was a dreary looking place.

It was too late to do anything that evening, the one we arrive at the river in. But the next morning the wagons went back, and we went to work to cork and pitch our boat, and make general preparations for the proposed trip. Yes, and there was another boat with six men that I had forgotten about, called the Shamrock. Mrs. Jennings, the wife of the man at St. Thomas who had furnished us with lumber to build our boats and such other supplies as she had, when we had got our boats built, christened them, calling the Irish boys' the Shamrock, ours, the Lady Jennings, and the other one the Anna, her given name.

The Shamrock boys, having gone right to work all hands the morning before, was nearly ready to start. Their boat that night being in the river, the first one launched, but said that they would wait for us and all start together. So that night we all had our boats in the river ready for loading. Dulin, by steady hard work, had succeeded, although having no one to help him, the others standing around whittling, talking, or off fishing, in getting his boat ready and seemed to be as anxious as any one of us to go up the Canyon. But all of his partners had long faces and but little to say to us fellows who seemed to be bent on going. Although there had not been a word said by anyone about turning back. Still it was plain enough that all but Dulin, of the Anna wanted to, and was only waiting for somebody to propose it when they would sanction it too quick.

And the next morning, just as we was getting ready to load our boat, and they was still setting around the fire, an Indian came with a letter from Jennings at St. Thomas, stating that the Cook party had got back after getting up in the canyon as far as the mouth of the Diamond River, where they had left their boat and such things that was too heavy for them to carry and gone into Arizona until they had struck the old Beal Trail and had followed that to Beal Springs, then to Mineral Park, the Mouth of the Virgin River, home. And had found nothing, but had found it very hard and dangerous getting up the Canyon and advised us all to come back. Well, their faces brightened right up as if they had struck a rich prospect. Just what they wanted. The Cook's party was all good prospectors. All on the work and had worked on Snake River where it was all flour gold on the bars, just as it was there if there was any.

Before any of my party had a chance to speak, I turned loose. I says, "Don't let us turn back, boys, without giving it a trial. We have gone to a great deal of expense in outfitting and have got four month's provisions and what can we do with it. There is no place to sell it. Besides the boat, it will be a dead loss, for we can't eat it, nor do anything but leave it. Besides there is a large party here; take us all horsemen and all. And we don't know what they might have found. Nor but what they might have had some object in sending such word under the circumstances. Their grub must have been pretty short by this time, if not altogether, and had to come in to get more, and had found good prospects but couldn't stay to work them. And on coming in and finding that there was such a crowd going, had sent that word to discourage us to turn us back. And I am 'not' going back."

Well, they said we will give it a trial, and to work we went to loading the boat. The Shamrock boys saw that we was going to go up the Canyon, so they loaded up and went. While we was loading, Dulin came and sat down close to us and he looked awful blue. His face was as long as my arm. His party had all backed out, so he couldn't go. He hove a long sigh, one that came clear up from his boots and said he was sorry that his party had backed out for he was very anxious to get up the river, but didn't suppose there was any chance of going with us. I said that I had no objections if our boat had only been a little bigger. He said his boat was larger, we could take that and leave ours, if that was all. Which we all agreed to do and loaded his boat, the "Lady Jennings," and left the "Anna" on the sand bank.

And with a little flag with "Good Hope" on it, struck in the bow, took the letter the Indian had brought and with the Shamrock along side of us, started up the river. And when we got to where the horsemen was camped, Oliver got up on a rock and read the letters to the crowd and they all turned back to a man, which left us and the Shamrock in possession of the field.

Just below the mouth of the Canyon about a half a mile, is a long riffle, not very rough but with a very strong current, and about the center of it on the south side of the river, the one we was going on was a large rock, a few hundred feet in size. Or it was a portion of a cement hill that had become detached and had fallen into the river. And the current being so strong, made it rather a hard place to get around. Although we went by it all right, and we was ahead of the Shamrock and had got over the riffle or rapids, as it is most generally called, and was all in the boat just going to enter the Canyon, which is like going into or through a narrow gate in a very high wall. And as I was one of the rowers at that time, and was looking down the river, I saw one of the Shamrock boys jump upon a rock and swing his hat and was acting in an excited manner generally. I says, "There must be something wrong with the Shamrock, and we had better land, go down and see." Which we did, and all this the fellow with the hat was coming up towards us just a sailing and as soon as he got in hearing distance, he helloed to Oliver, who was ahead. "Oliver, the Shamrock is sunk, and all is going to hell. And if yee's will set us across the river so that we can go back, we will be much obleedged to yee's."

We walked along down with him, and he was giving the trip fits and anybody connected with it, in his Irish brogue, which was somewhat amusing. Although for them, very unfortunate, and when we got to the rock, sure enough the Shamrock, in trying to get around that rock, had upset and everything that they had that would float was going, dancing over the waves, down the river. Blankets, clothes, all such things was strung along down the river as far as the eye could see. They had saved nothing, only their lives and the boat. And one poor fellow had taken off his clothes, down to an undershirt and drawers, which was all he had. But we rigged him out with a shirt and pair of pants, and as they still had their boat, they said that they didn't need us, for as soon as they got it bailed out, they would all get into it, run down to where they started from that morning and the next day go to St. Thomas, as it was only about forty miles from the river. They could easily make it in a day.

So we left them and going back to our boat, I looked back and there they were in the boat on the back tract, leaving us alone, the five of us out of about two hundred that had started out. And from then on there seemed to be a kind of a dampness to our feelings. We wasn't as jovial and lively as had been all the fore part of the day, and I don't think there was one of us that wanted to turn back, or would have listened to it had it been proposed. Still there seemed to be a cloud over us, and when we got to the boat, we camped, although it early in the evening, instead of going into the Canyon as we had calculated on before the misfortune of the Shamrock. And that evening talking around the campfire, which blazed up high and cheerful as if trying to dispel the gloom that had apparently settled on our hearts as if of some approaching evil was shadowing our footsteps and which very plainly affected us all. Although none spoke of it and the only anything like an allusion to it was that Dulin said, "Let us go slow but sure and above all not get anyone drowned."

Little did he think, setting on that log of driftwood, the bright light of the fire shining on his honest face, as like the rest of us, he was trying to force a cheerfulness to dispel the foreboding spirit misfortune that he was uttering a warning that ten days from that time was going to be fulfilled to the letter.

The next day, and for ten of them, we crawled up into that canyon under those towering cliffs that for thousands of feet rear their tops towards the stars entirely shutting out the sun from casting its shadow on the river below. Shutting us off, as it were, from all civilization, leaving the world of life behind and entering a realm in which animal life was still unknown. For the only living things we saw was two crows that followed us up the river. And on our leaving camp would fly down and pick up whatever they could find to eat.

Many times going up the canyon on those rapids, working along with the boat trying to work it around the rocks, that my feet was swept from under me. But by good luck or something else would always manage to grab hold of the boat or something that always seemed to be around and some times looked as if it was there just for that purpose. And we would stop along and prospect where ever there was a bar that we thought was likely to have any gold on it. And sometimes got very good fine gold prospects, but the bars was very small and very little dirt, mostly all rocks, so that it took a great deal of ground as the fellows said to make a little dirt. And I noticed the best prospects was in the edge of the water. The lower we could get in the river, the better the prospect. But it was the wrong time of the year. It should have been late in the summer, instead of early April, for the river was constantly rising from the melting snows in the mountains further up and towards the source of the river.

But we got along very well until that day, the 10th of April, and close to the head of a heavy rapids and where the river was confined to a narrow channel. There was a large granite boulder, oblong in shape, and I suppose twenty feet long, lay with one end in the bar and the rest out in that boiling current, making a very bad place to take a loaded boat. And had we unloaded the boat, I don't think we would have had any difficulty. But we didn't and although there was four of us a pulling on the line when she took that current, jerked us all in a pile, pulled the rope away from us and down the river she went, leaving us there in that canyon, in a hostile Indian country afoot. Nor could we see any way to get out. The walls rose up on all sides without an apparent break, which when there was, would be from some wash that would run into the canyon and which could sometimes be followed out and by that means get out of the canyon, and in most places without a boat the only means of getting out.

But the boat didn't go far before she anchored by, I suppose the rope drawing in between the rocks and a large knot in the end prevented it from drawing through, holding it in the river not far from the opposite bank. In the fall, Dulin hurt his knee, and I was standing talking to him when the other boys, picking up the oars that lay on the bar, sung out to me as they started up the river to watch the boat and that they would go up the river, build a raft out of drift wood, cross the river, come down on the opposite side and get the boat. Dulin says to me that I had better go down and watch the boat. "It might tear loose at any time and as soon as my knee gets well, I will go up the river somewhere and swim over."

For a little while, I tried to persuade him out of the notion for the water was very cold and there was a cold wind blowing up the canyon. But he seemed confident of his ability to swim it, so I left him and taking my rifle went down on a point below the boat where I could see up and down the river for a mile or so and the boat at the same time. I hadn't been there but a few minutes before I saw George Magil come down on the opposite side of the river to where the boat was, but thought it was Dulin, and I could see by his actions that he could do nothing. Then that he was over there and at about the same time Charlie Goodnow came down on my side of the river and sat down on a rock opposite the boat. And by this time I thought that the boat was there to stay, I would go and see what was going to be done and what had become of Dulin and Oliver. When I got to where Charlie was, I saw then that it was George that had swam the river instead of Dulin. And I wanted to know of Charlie what had become of the other two. He said that they was going to swim the river with the oars. At the same time, I saw Oliver come running down the river as if the devil was after him. And with premonitions of something wrong, we started to meet him, and he said that Dulin was drowned.

On the opposite side of the river from a little above the boat, up the river about a mile and a half, a mile above the rapids was a cliff three or four hundred feet high, a wall from the water's edge to the top. Then there was a shelf thirty or forty feet wide that when once on it, there was no trouble in getting along and about a half a mile above the rapids was a landing, a break in the cliff where it was easy to climb up on to the top. And at the break was a sand bar twenty or thirty feet long. But if that landing was missed by anyone trying to swim the river, they never would get out in the world because before they could anywhere near get back, the suction from the rapids would take them over. George, when he swam it, he went high up the river and took a good start on it and had plenty of room and made it all right. But he said it was all he could do.

Dulin and Oliver undertook it with the oars, but didn't go far enough up the river and found before they had gone far that they was drifting too fast to make the landing, so came back. When Dulin tried it again without any oars or waiting to get warm again and didn't go high enough that time. And Oliver said before he had got three-fourths of the distance across, he had drifted below the landing and was under that cliff when he sunk and nearly across as near as he could tell. But no possible chance for him to get out or save himself.

George was over there but could do nothing. But Charlie managed to throw his butcher knife over to him. Then from a pile of drift a little below, he got a long pole, tied the butcher knife to it and cut the rope close to where it was tied to the boat. When it ran down a short distance to a short turn in the river and where there was an eddy, he swam in and got it, took out one of the seats and with a hatchet, made a paddle and came back to the side we was on.

But our rope was gone and without a rope, it was impossible to get our boat up over the rapids. So we had to come away and leave Dulin in the river. We could go up on the top of the cliff and look down at the place where Oliver thought he sank but we could see nothing. The river is always muddy and very much so in the spring. There seemed to be an eddy where he sank so no doubt he is there yet. For they say the Colorado River never gives up its dead. But it seemed so hard to have come away and leave him there in the river without trying to get him out, but what could we do? We couldn't get our boat up there, and without a boat it was impossible to get to where he had sunk. And to lose a comrade in that out of the way, wild, terrible, dismal place was too horrible to think about. And I imagined I could hear him calling not to leave him. Friends may die surrounded with comfort of Brothers or Sisters where they can see the flowers and trees or at least fields of level country and cause us a great deal of grief. But to die in that dark and life forsaken place and be left there was more appalling I believe than it is possible for it to occur in any other way or place.

But it had to be done and the next morning we got into our boat and ran part of the way down and a strong head wind rose so that we was afraid to run for fear we might, in some of the rapids, where the waves run pretty high, get upset. So we had to lay up until the next day. And then before we got down to where we started, we came near being wrecked. We was running a rapids and George, who was lookout, I and Oliver rowing, and Charlie steering, when

The Grand Canyon

George yelled, "To the right, to the right, a rock." Which was just in time, for the boat raked it as it went flying past. One inch more and it would at least have stove a hole in her if not mashed or upset. But we passed it alright. But I tell you, it was a close shave. We got down about noon that day and that night went to St. Thomas getting in the morning for breakfast. And I reported Dulin's death by a sworn statement before a notary, who happened to be there at the time and who said would have it published in a Pioche paper as soon as he got there. Then we rented a wagon out and brought in the other two boys and that ended that trip. Lost a man and never made a single quarter.

I dont believe that a centipedes feet are poison, at least
to have one crawl over you wont hurt you. for I had
it tried on me once, I dont know what might ha
happened had I hurt it. so that it had have
stuck its feet into my flesh as they say. it
does when either frightened or hurt. and then
I doubt it for they have fangs, and that is
where I think their poison comes from.

It was at Tueson in the summer of 77. and
in that country they grow pretty large. for
I have seen them that measured ten
inches, Where I had been with some ore
from where the Tombstone district is now
and I had been carrying it around town
to see iff I couldent get somebody interest
but it was no go. with very few exception
they wouldent look at it and those that did
pronounced it very low grade, And a man
that, at that time would have put up $150. or
$200 would have owned half of Tombstone. for
with that much money. then. I could have
found eny mine there was in Tombstone
off eny account. because there was no Prospectors in the country. and before anybody
had have found it out. I would have had
them all.

Well as I said I had been poking around
all day. and had met with no encourag

CHAPTER 8

BY THE
LIGHT OF
THE STARS

I don't believe that a centipede's feet are poison, at least to have one crawl over you won't hurt you, for I had it tried on me once. I don't know what might have happened had I hurt it so that it had have stuck its feet into my flesh as they say it does when either frightened or hurt. And then I doubt it, for they have fangs and that is where I think their poison comes from.

It was at Tucson in the summer of '77, and in that country they grow pretty large, for I have seen them that measured ten inches where I had been with someone from where the Tombstone district is now. And I had been carrying it around town to see if I couldn't get somebody interested. But it was no go. With very few exceptions they wouldn't look at it and those that did pronounced it very low grade. And a man that at that time would have put up $150 or

$200 would have owned half of Tombstone, for with that much money then I could have found any mine there was in Tombstone of any account, because there was no prospectors in the country and before anybody had have found them out, I would have had them all.

Well, as I said, I had been poking around all day and met with no encouragement and had gone back to camp on a mesquite flat on the bank of the Santa Cruz River, a little way above Tucson. And had gone to bed. Had taken the most of my clothes off as it was very warm and no danger from Indians. I was making myself as comfortable as possible under the circumstances and was laying there star gazing with only one blanket partially drawn over me and wondering what was the next best thing for me to do, and I had found that Tucson was no place for a prospector. At least not for me. When I felt something run up onto my left leg below the knee and start down for my feet which was naked, my drawers covering my legs, and going as if it was in a hurry. Throwing the blanket off, just as it was going over my feet, by the light of the stars, I saw it was a large centipede, and it felt large. I thought at the time and as I raised out of those blanket, like a flash of lightening, that it was two feet long and weighed a ton. And for a while I was scared and was on the point of going to the Doctor but kept waiting for it to hurt, which it failed to do. But it passed over both of my feet and excepting the scare I got, which of course only lasted a few minutes, I felt nothing of it. Nor did it show any signs next morning where it had been on them.

In the summer of 77. when
Griffith Smith and myself was
doing the assessment work on
the Bronkow mine. just previous
to the discovery of Tombstone. we
had quite an adventure, and one
I will never forget-

We were camped on the San
Pedro, about half a mile from
where the town of Charleston was
afterwards built,- and where the
trail from Cochises stronghold
crosses the river, running through
a large thickett of willows.

One evening shortly after we had
returned from the mine, I and
Griffith was fishing. while Smith
was laying down in camp. when
happening to glance down the river,
I saw, a smoke just rising. evidently
from a fire just kindled! dropping
fish pole as iff it had have beede
a hot poker, I ran to camp. and
there lay Smith about half asleep
with his gun setting up against
the small ash tree that grew there
solitary and a lone. serving us
for a shade in the absence of a

CHAPTER 9

PLACE IN THE WILLOWS

In the summer of '77 when Griffith Smith and myself was doing the assessment work on the Brunckow mine, just previous to the discovery of Tombstone, we had quite an adventure and one I will never forget.

We were camped on the San Pedro, about half a mile from where the town of Charleston was afterwards built, and where the trail from Cochise's stronghold crosses the river running through a large thicket of willows.

One evening, shortly after we had returned from the mine, I and Griffith was fishing while Smith was laying down in camp when happening to glance down the river, I saw a smoke just rising, evidently for a fire just kindled. Dropping fish pole as if it had have been a hot poker, I ran to camp and there lay Smith about half asleep with his gun setting up against the small ash tree that grew there solitary and alone, serving us for a shade in the absence of a tent.

"What's that smoke just started down there in the willows on the trail?" I exclaimed. "Don't know. It must be Indians." "Well, let us go and see." So taking his gun, mine always being in my hands, and when eating, across my lap, we slipped cautiously along the bank through the tall grass and low willows that grew along the sides, keeping our eyes open, and out of sight, but always so that we could see the place in the willows where the smoke was slowly raising in a small spiral column. The very embodiment of a novelist's Indian fire.

Finally we reached a place where we could see down under the willows, close to the water's edge. And there, in a spot clear of brush, about ten feet square, sat an Indian. And Smith raised his gun to shoot him. "Hold on Smith," I says. "Hold on, hold on. Don't be too fast. He hasn't seen us yet. Nor I can't see but the one, and there may be a hundred of them in those willows. So wait a while and if there are any more, some of them will certainly show themselves very soon. In the meantime, we can watch this one's actions and determine what course to pursue. He can't get away from us. Besides he might be a Mexican."

"A Mexican? The devil, what would a Mexican be doing there, and naked. That fellow hasn't even got his blanket around him. He is one of old Cochise's damned Indians, and I am going to shoot him."

"No you don't. No shooting to be done here yet awhile until I know more about him. Well, let's call him up to us."

"All right. We can step out so that he can see us and see that we are white men, and I'll cover him with my gun so that if he makes a break to get away, I can kill him. And if he should be a Mexican, he will be only too glad to see us. And if an Indian, and sees that he is covered and can't get away, he may come to us and once get a hold of him then we are safe."

When we stepped out in full view, I drew my gun on him, full cocked and Smith hailed him, at the same time motioned for him to come to us. Raising his head and seeing two white men standing out in plain view, armed with repeating rifles and one of them pointing directly at him, he must have thought the chances of running away was very slim, and that he had better come and see what we wanted.

So rising up showing that he was perfectly naked and throwing his blanket around himself, came very indifferently slowly along to where we were. At the same time, Griff, who had heard Smith hollering, had run to camp and seeing the smoke rising from the willows, I and Smith down that way and an Indian coming towards us, came running down to see what was up. He and the Indian both getting there at the same time.

And turning to me, said, "Sheff, there are white men among these Indians. That fellow is no Indian, he is a white man." And stepping up to him, asked him what he was doing in that country in the condition that he was in. As from appearances, he evidently was naked and if he had any arms, none being visible, but his blanket was wrapped around him and his hands underneath having the appearance of having a six-shooter in one of them and waiting an opportunity to use it. For in answering Griff, he was impudent, telling him that it was none of his business whether he had any arms or not, or what he was doing in the country.

Then Griff told him that we was in a dangerous place, in a bad Indian country, that his appearances created suspicion and that we wanted he should camp with us that night. That we would treat him well but for our own protection under the circumstances not knowing who he was, we wanted him to raise his blanket and let us see whether he had any arms or not. And that if he had, he must give them up until morning when we would return them as we got them.

Reluctantly, he raised his blanket, showing that he was without arms, and with the exception of a part of one leg of a pair of pants, he was entirely naked, hatless and his feet wrapped up in burley sacks. His skin sunburnt and badly tanned from exposure until he looked as much like an Indian as it was possible for a man to and not be one. His single badly worn blanket, doing the double duty of clothes and for a bed, an old frying pan without any handle and about ten pounds of flour completed his outfit.

Amongst us that evening, we fitted him out with clothes, minus hat and boots, not having any of those, only what we was wearing. But looked more comfortable and much more presentable the next morning when he started for Camp Huachuca, after thanking us very profusely, where he stopped for a few days, then started across the mountains for Santa Cruz, Mexico. And that was the last I ever heard of him. In talking with him, I found him a well educated man and that his name, so he said, was Timothy Malloy, and that was all. He would give no further account of himself. And that his reason for being in such a destitute condition was that he was unable to obtain employment. The last place that he had worked was for John Sizemore in Jackson County, Oregon. That after leaving there, he had kept coming south until he had spent all of his money and was in the condition that we saw him. And that he had become disgusted with the Americans and was now going to Sonora and make his home with the Mexicans. He had heard that they was very hospitable and kind to strangers.

The conclusions that we came to was that he was an escaped lunatic but had sense enough, as he had no canteen and no means of carrying water, to follow the rivers. And a year or so afterwards, when I was down at the mouth of the San Pedro, I heard of him. When he came to a cabin, if there was no one around, he would go in, eat all there was cooked, and sometimes there would be enough for three or four men, it made no difference. He either eat it all or took it with him, but the general supposition was that he ate it, for he would always take a few pounds of flour (but disturb nothing else) accounting for the flour that he had with him when we saw him.

Talk about the freaks of fortune, and off
the chances that men have, and min
I will tell you of an instance that
came under my observation, in
fact—I was one of the parties

When I was prospecting in the
Tombstone county, and just before
its discovery. One night, about
thirty miles from Tombstone,
on the San Pedro river, where I was
camped. W. T. Griffith. And Alva
Smith. came there. on their
way. to the Old Bronkow Mine.
on which they was going to do
the assessment work. And it
being a very bad place. for Ind
-ians. And as I had a good sharp
rifle. six shooter. plenty of ammuni
-tion and a field glass. that
I would be a good hand to
stand guard while they worked.
which was proposed to me. and
which I accepted,

The next day we went down
the river to where Charleston
now is. and about a mile from
the Bronkow. And where we
camped on account of water.
there being no water at the

CHAPTER 10

FREAKS OF FORTUNE

Talk about the freaks of fortune and of the chances that men have and miss, I will tell you of an instance that came under my observation. In fact I was one of the parties.

When I was prospecting in the Tombstone country and just before its discovery, one night about thirty miles from Tombstone on the San Pedro River, where I was camped, W.T. Griffith and Alva Smith came there on their way to the Old Brunckow Mine on which they was going to do the assessment work. And it being a very bad place for Indians and as I had a good sharp rifle, six-shooter, plenty of ammunition and a field glass, that I would be a good hand to stand guard while they worked, which was proposed to me and which I accepted.

The next day, we went down the river to where Charleston now is and about a mile from the Brunckow and where we camped on account of water, there being no water at the mine. And after the work was done, Griff had found that I was there in that country expressly for prospecting for I had not mentioned a ranch. While him and Smith had both picked out places to take up ranches as they was coming down, and as we was going back up the river to where they was going to locate their ranches. Griff proposed to me that if I would locate him, not as a partner, but locate a claim for him, at the same time, and joining mine, that he would furnish me with provisions, have the recording done and what assaying that was necessary. He having a team with which he could make money enough for that purpose. And which I agreed to do in this way. That if he would do as he proposed, whenever I found anything I thought worth locating, that before doing so I would let him know it. Then one of us build the monument at the places of discovery, and the other take choice of claims, which was better and suited him better, than the proposition that he had made.

A day or two after that and after they had staked out their ranches of one hundred and sixty acres each, him and Smith went to Tucson to get provisions, the money for their work on the mine, and some tools that they wanted to build cabins and to work their ranches. And was gone about two weeks, and I was there when they came back. And Griff says, "Sheff, I have heard you say often that fortune knocks at a man's door once in a life time. I think it is knocking at mine now." (At the time there was a law called the Desert Act by which a man could locate six hundred acres of land if he would reclaim it by putting water on it.) "There is a man in Tucson that says that if I can find a good piece of land out here, to take it up under the Desert Act, and he will furnish money for me to put water on it. And I am going to do it. It is a disappointment to you, for our agreement will fall through for I can't do both. But it is a chance that I am not going to let pass."

"Alright, Griff," I said, "you know your own business best, but I think that you will miss it." But they paid me for standing guard and the next morning Griff started down the river with his team looking for a ranch. And on a mesquite bottom about four miles above where Benson now stands, on the San Pedro, he took up his six hundred acres, stayed there about a month when the Indians got to killing people all around the country. Loaded up, went into Tucson, stayed there a few days and then went up to the neighborhood of the McCracken Mines and spent the winter. Then in the spring, when the excitement broke out about the Tombstone mines, he went back to where Contention City is now and him and a man by the name of Bruno went to raising pumpkins for the very mines, that had he have carried out his proposition, he would of owned one half. But he had not only lost them but his desert ranch too.

About that time, he was in Tucson one day when somebody wanted him to claim a half interest with me in all my mines under that agreement. But he wouldn't do it. He said it was all his own fault. That I had acted perfectly honorable with him and he should by me. That if he had have done as I wanted him to do he would have had just as many and just as good claims as I had. But by his own act, he had thrown the chance away, and nobody but himself was to blame for it. So when we sold out, I gave him five thousand dollars for his honesty and he sold out, went to Virginia, his old home, calculating to start a tobacco store. But I never heard from him.

The history of the discovery of Tombstone
and how it was named

In march 1877 I was prospecting
in the Walaipai country along the line
of where the Atlantic Pacific. R.R. now
runs. when a company of the Walaipai
Indians were inlisted, to go too the
southern part of the Territory. on a scou
-ting expedition. against the Chirri chuman
Apaches. who was committing depredations
whenever the oppertunity presented its self
Thinking that there was a good oppertun
-ity for prospecting, by going with them.
for they would afford me protection. I
went along. but not as a scout as many
supposes. Arriving at Camp Hauchuca
about the first of April. where the scouts
remained. for some time. recruiting
and making preprations for the summ
-ers campaign. during that time I would
take trips through the country. notwith
standing the warnings I received from
the soldiers, of the danger of going a
lone. and on my returns would ask
iff I had found anything. which I had
not. You will. they would say you'll find
your tombstone iff you dont stop running
through this country. all alone as you are

CHAPTER 11

MY TOMBSTONE

Tⁱhe history of the discovery of Tombstone and how it was named.

In March 1877, I was prospecting in the Walaipai Country along the line of where the Atlantic Pacific R.R. now runs, when a company of the Walaipai Indians were enlisted to go to the southern part of the Territory on a scouting expedition against the Chirichuhua Apaches who was committing depredations whenever the opportunity presented itself. Thinking that there was a good opportunity for prospecting by going with them, for they would afford me protection, I went along. But not as a scout as many supposes, arriving at Camp Huachuca about the first of April where the scouts remained for some time recruiting and making preparations for the summer's campaign.

During that time, I would take trips through the country, notwithstanding the warnings I received from the soldiers of the danger of going alone, and on my return would ask if I had found anything, which I had not. You will, they would say. You'll find your Tombstone if you don't stop running through this country all alone as you are while the Indians are so bad. The remarks being made often impressed the name on my mind, so much so that the first mine of any importance that I found, I called it Tombstone thinking at the time of the vast difference in the one I had found, and the one referred to by the soldiers.

In May, the scouts started out to be gone twenty days and I with them. But it wasn't long before I discovered that a scouting party was no place for a prospector, and if I found anything, I must take the chances and go it alone for.they was hunting one thing and I another. Consequently, our movements were entirely different. So on their return, when they got to the San Pedro River, one day's march from the Post, they went on and I remained, not having found a color on the trip. After I had been there a day or two, one morning before daybreak, a couple of men came along who had contracted to do the assessment work on the Brunckow mine, about eight miles from where Tombstone now is. And seeing that I was well armed with plenty of ammunition, they proposed for me to go with them and stand guard while they worked. It being considered a very dangerous place for Indians and judging from numerous graves around, together with a trail from Cochise's stronghold passing over the mine, I thought their considerations correct and very suggestive of finding a Tombstone.

After finishing there, we moved up the river a few miles where some others joined us and all but me took up ranches, which they thought very strange. And afterwards when I had found rich ores and tried to explain and show them the metal in them, they would look upon me with pity and say they hoped so, and that I had better give the prospecting up and take up a ranch. That I would make more, and that if I found anything, I could do nothing with it for it took capital

Sonoran Desert in southern Arizona

to work a mine. And I don't know what objections they didn't raise, nor during the time that we were together none of them would ever go with me to look at my prospects, about twenty five miles from there. I camped with them because I dared not camp in the Tombstone hills on account of its nearness to Cochise's stronghold. In fact during the time that I was prospecting in there that summer, not once did I build a fire. I would ride in early in the morning taking a lunch and canteen of water with me, picket my mule near where I was at work. And she was always on the alert, better than a dog, and seemed to have a realization of the danger she was in, always saddled with the bridle hanging to the horn. Rifle in one hand and pick the other, cartridge belt and six-shooter around me day or night just the same. After doing so for a while, I would pack up and go off to some other part of the country for a week or so, return and try it again and so on all summer.

In August, being out of provisions, no clothes and only five dollars in money, which in those days was none at all, I took some ore and went to Tucson to see what I could do, and I very soon found out. For they would neither look at me or the ore and said that they didn't want any mines. Government contracts and Posts was good enough for them and that a man was foolish to be spending his time looking for imaginary fortunes. He ought to be at work somewhere. Go take up a ranch and be somebody. That if he found anything it would do him no good, for it took capital to work mines and before capital would invest there had to be a great deal of work done to show what they were, which all took money. And one house that not long after failed, gave me to understand that, unless I had the money, not to come there for anything. For if I did, I wouldn't get it. And I wanted a sack of flour damned bad, but as I hadn't the money, I didn't go. Nor haven't been yet. So I had to go back, as I came, only a little mad and more determined.

A few miles from camp I met a man named Sampson who was going prospecting for placer mines and wanted me to go with him. And as the Indians were on the warpath again, having killed sixteen not far from there a day or two before, and all the boys leaving the river going to the different Posts, making the future look rather gloomy for me, agreed to go. He furnishing the grub. Next day we went to Camp Huachuca where I got my mules shod, having thirty cents left after paying for the shoeing. Then we struck out and was gone twenty-one or -two days and never found a color.

When we got back to the river, it was entirely deserted. Not a soul on it, and Sampson, disgusted with the country, struck out for South America. But he didn't go far, for I saw him a year or two afterwards, which left me without grub again, and he had none to divide for we had eaten it nearly all up on the trip. But I had a good rifle and plenty of

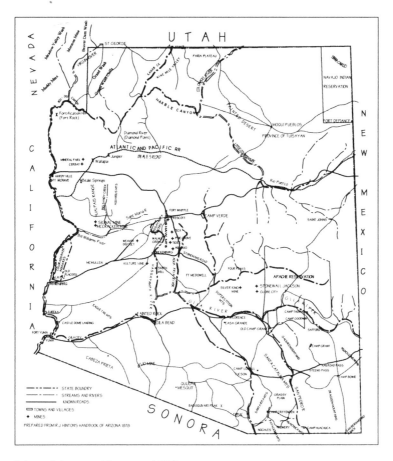

Map of Arizona Territory, 1872

ammunition and game very plentiful, deer or antelope in sight constantly all day long. So I was all right, but there was no use for me to stay there any longer. I had found a good mining camp but no money to have any records made, so there was no use to make any locations. The truth of the matter is I had no paper to write the notices on nor enough money to buy it with.

And after studying the matter over, ragged with Indians committing depredations on all sides and hard up generally, I concluded the best thing for me to do was to see if I couldn't find my brother, Al, who was somewheres in the Territory. The last I had heard from him, he was at the Silver King eight months before. But where was he then? The Silver King was the place to go. If he wasn't there, I could get on his trail and track him up.

So for the King two hundred miles away through a hostile Indian country I started, keeping in the mountains and away from roads and trails to avoid being ambushed. And then one day came near meeting them while riding up a canyon where there was a spring of water and not seeing any Indian signs until I got close to the spring. Where the first thing I saw was their camp, but it was too late to turn back. So rode slowly on ready to fire at the first one that showed himself. But they were all away, and being a war party there was no squaws with them to give an alarm. And by riding until late in the night, they couldn't track me up.

And when I got to Globe City, thirty miles from the King, I met a man that had been at work there, and he said that they had discharged a lot of men, Al amongst them, and that he had gone to the McCracken mine two hundred miles north. And as my mules was sore footed and no money to get them shod, the best thing was to go to work. But where to get a job. There was but very little doing there and the town full of idle men. The Stonewall Jackson mine, a few miles from there, had just been sold to a California company and they were working quite a number of men. Thinking my chances were better, I went over there and there met some boys whom I was acquainted with that had been waiting for a chance to go work for nearly a month and was then making adobes. Making about enough to pay for their board by cooking it themselves and sleeping in their own tent waiting their turn for the promised job in the mine to come. Notwithstanding all that, I asked the foreman if he couldn't put me to work at something. But he said no. That he was refusing men every day looking for work. Well, it was no use to stay there. Game was scarce, and I hadn't had a square meal in so long that I was getting pretty slim.

So I packed up and started again, not knowing where to go. But took the trail back for Globe by way of the Champion mine, three miles from the Stonewall. And met the foreman coming down the hill going to the boarding house. And asked him for a job. I told him I had to have work. He surveyed me from head to foot a few times before he said anything. And I guess I was a hard looking citizen for my clothes, what was left of them, was tied with strings and patched with pieces of blankets, gunny sacks or anything else I had been able to get ahold of. And the patches had worn out. "Well," he said, "judging from your looks, you do need a job and that, very bad. I have no tools for to put you in the mine, but you can go to work on the windlass at nights. Not a very good job, nor very good pay. Three dollars a night and you can get your meals at the boarding house, but you will have to furnish your own blankets, which I suppose you have with you." A poor job under any other circumstance, standing and turning a windlass all night, snowing the most of the time, without shelter, for three dollars. And thirteen of them was enough. All the money I wanted. My mules was shod and rested, I had clean clothes on, grub enough to last me to McCracken mines and seventy-five cents in money. What more did I want?

When I got to the McCracken mines, I found Al at work in the Signal mine and showed him what ore I had with me. And like all the others that had seen it, said it was low grade. Well, I couldn't prove that it wasn't, for I had not been able to have any assay made. And only had my own judgments to go on and that against everybody else's. Still I wouldn't believe but what it was good ore, but we didn't argue the question. The foreman wanted a man to fill buckets. So I went to work that night and not long after that Dick Gird came up to the mine as an assayer and Al being acquainted with him, got him to assay my ore. It running from forty to two thousand dollars a ton and a very easy ore to work. Still Al didn't say anything about going down with me. But Dick wanted to go, and I wanted Al. And it was some time before I could get him in the notion. But at last he concluded to go.

So we all threw up our jobs. Dick got a mule and a light wagon, an assay outfit and with my old guard, Beck, harnessed with Dick's, we left Signal the fourteenth of February about noon and got to the Brunckow mine on the twenty-sixth, where we camped for about three weeks. Then built us a shanty out of the stalks of a specie of cactus, using the wagon cover for a roof. No Indians being in Cochise's stronghold, old Cochise having died there a short time before and his Indians, thinking it bad medicine, had all left for other parts of the Territory. So that it was comparatively safe.

When we left Signal, there was another party left a few days before us, and nobody knew where they was going. Nor no one but me, and I wouldn't tell, knew where we was going, and at all the stations on the road to Tucson, we could hear of them, and it began to look as if they had found out where we was going. They all being acquainted with Dick and thinking he had something pretty good and was going to be there with him until we reached the San Pedro River and at the station, at the crossing, and there they were, but all but one was out in the hills, and he heard us go by. But it was a very cold windy disagreeable day and, being sick, he wouldn't get up to look out to see who it was. Nor did we stop, although we had calculated to before we saw their wagon. Then we hurried by as soon as possible for we wanted nobody to follow us or be there until we had made our locations and those of the best. And having to labor under so many disadvantages the summer before, I was

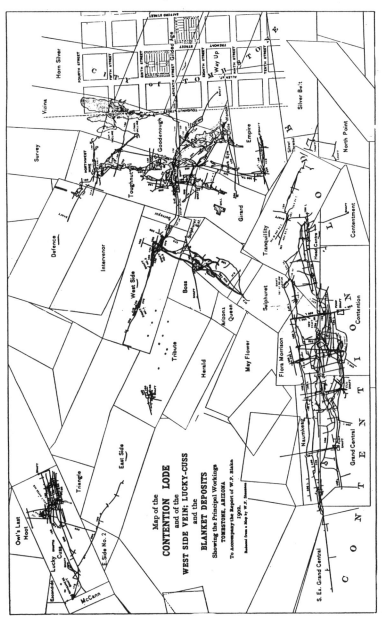

Map of the Contention Lode

satisfied that I had not found the best mines, and after taking chances to hunt the country out and find the district, I didn't want somebody else to come in and get the richest mines. And one of them told me afterwards that if he had of seen us and Dick being along that he would have followed sure.

While camped at the Brunckow and before we had been there long, possibly a week, the mines that we had found up to that time wasn't of no very great importance, and Dick says one day, "Suppose we load up and go over to the Chirichuhuas where those other fellows must have went. They must have had something pretty good to come all the way, not only from Signal, but from San Francisco down here to this country." So I saddled up old Beck and went into the Dragoon Mountains where Cochise's stronghold is and was gone a couple of days. And when going back, not far from where the town of Tombstone is now, and on the Westside mine, but at that time was not discovered, I stopped and took a good look at the hills and the formations and made up my mind that if there wasn't good mines somewhere in that neighborhood, there was no use of judging from indications, or experiences amounted to nothing. For if that wasn't a mineral country, I had never seen one. And that if Dick was still in the notion of going to the Chirichuhuas he could take his part of the outfit and go, but I would stay where I was. And a day or two after that I found the Lucky Cuss. Then there was no more talk of going away.

Hank Williams and Jack Oliver, a couple of prospectors whose animals ran away from them and one of them about fifteen miles from there and one got in with ours, and when they found it, seeing that we were prospectors with an outfit for assaying, thought they would try it for awhile. As our assays showed that there was good ore there and after a couple weeks prospecting and not finding anything, got discouraged and was going to leave when Dick persuaded

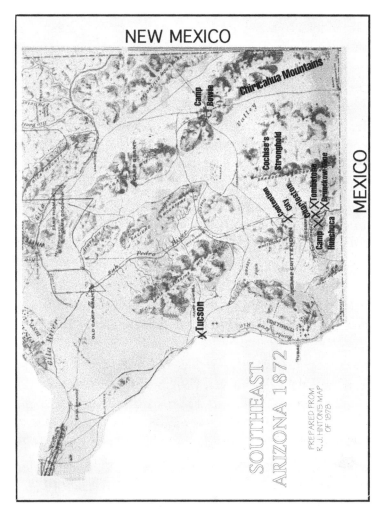

Map of Southern Arizona

them to try it awhile longer. The result of which was they found the Grand Central. One of the best mines in the district and one we could have had and would had Dick let them go when they wanted to.

And as soon as they found it, one of them went to Camp Huachuca, got drunk and told of the discovery which created an excitement. And the party that was in the Chirichuhuas, White Parsons and Smith hearing of it came in there and we sold the Contention mine to White for ten thousand dollars. And not long afterwards bonded our other mines to Charles Lozies for San Francisco parties for ninety thousand, giving him ninety days to make the sale or lose the forfeit of five thousand dollars that he had put up. The time given in the bond expiring and no sale, we went to work on the mines and had been at work about two months when Sam Safford came in, and we gave him a fourth interest in our principal mines for putting up a ten stamp mill. He, in order to raise the money, interested the Corbins of Connecticut and by the 1st of June the following year (79), the mill was running.

And not being able to make arrangements with the stage company, that by this time was running daily, to carry our bullion on account of the dangers from robbers, Mexicans and Indians, we had to take it to Tucson ourselves. And as Al was in the east trying to sell stock and Dick had to be at the mill all the time and somebody directly interested had to go with it, it fell to me. So with four good mules, a thorough brace wagon, driver, two guards on horseback, one hundred yards or so ahead, and the other the same distance behind, while I was on the wagon making two shipments a month without once being molested. Notwithstanding the warnings we repeatedly got and of the danger universally conceded by everybody in making such large shipments at that time so close to the line of Mexico, where in case of robbery, they could get in a few hours' ride.

In November, Al returning from the East and Wells Fargo Co. having an office in Tombstone and running messengers, shipping our bullion through them, I packed up and went out prospecting for about four months. On my returning, I found a party from Phil. (Philadelphia) in Tombstone who wanted I and Al's interest which we let them have for $600,000 each to be paid in monthly installments. The last one to be on the 1st of September. We retaining possession of the stock until the last payment.

July 11, 1884
San Francisco Chronicle
THE TOMBSTONE DISTRICT
An Interesting Talk with Its Discoverer.

"I think that the day will come when Arizona will produce more bullion than all the rest of our territory," said Edward Schieffelin to a *CHRONICLE* reporter the other day.

"What makes you think so?"

"There is mineral in every place you go. There is no place that you can strike without it having metal. The trouble is that there is too much Eastern capital in the Territory. You know the Eastern people go in heavily for science—they wish to do everything by science. Now this will not do. The territory wants men who will do things properly, and when it gets this class it will become a great mining country."

"You discovered Tombstone?"

"Oh, I was always prospecting and in one of these tours came across Tombstone."

"How did it get this name?"

"I was up in the northern part of the Territory, in that section known as the Wallapai country, and while there a company of Indians was enlisted for an Apache hunt in the southern part of the Territory, and I followed them down. During my journey I was several times asked if I had ever made anything in these prospecting tours, and I used to say that I had not discovered anything of very great value yet, but I hoped later on to do so. I was always alone when I made my prospects in the Apache country. This, no doubt, was dangerous, as the Apaches were very active about that time. They were killing men all over the country and had dispatched two or three trains that summer. Well, the soldiers often used to tell me to be careful and advise me not to venture out alone, telling me, among other things, 'Oh, yes, you'll find a tombstone one of these days; that is what you will find.' This remark was so often made that it impressed itself on my memory. And often when I was in these prospects it would unpleasantly recur, and at length I determined if I succeeded in finding anything to give it this name. Well, in the summer and fall of 1877, I entered the present Tombstone district, made my discoveries, but the locations were not made till the spring of 1878. The delay was owing to the Indians. My finds lay only nine miles from Cochise's stronghold and at that time I never built a fire in the district for fear of attracting the Indians. I used to stay there about a couple of days; go into other portions of the country for a week or so and then come back again. That fall I left the country, went to Tucson and tried to get the men there to take an interest in my Tombstone mines. But they would not listen to me. So I went and hunted up my brother (by this time Cochise was dead and the Apaches had scattered) and he, Dick Gird and I started for the new mines, where we arrived in February, 1878, and then made a camp out of bear grass poles, with a canvas stretched across them. We stayed there about six to eight months, then got some lumber and built a house, in which we lived till the spring of 1880, when I and my brother sold out our interests. Dick Gird retained his interests for another year."

"Do you intend to settle down now?"

"No, I detest city life. I am now on my way to Nevada, where I shall prospect again. If the country is what I think it is, I shall stay a few months; otherwise I shall not."

Little things, makes a felow feel awful good
some times. About the most pleased that
I ever was in my life. was an invitation
to dinner once

In the fall of 77. I was going from
the Tombstone country, to the Globe
district. and as the Indians was
very bad. I had kept in the mountains.
so as to avoid trails and roads. so
that they couldn't lay and wait for
me. And at the place I speak of
is where, I came down out of the
mountains onto the San Pedro River.
and from there folowed it down
to the Gila.

I guess it was about ten o'clock in
the morning that I got there. and
there was a woman, herding cows
out of the corn, and doing her house
work too. While her husband, with
some Mexicans, was husking and
hauling the corn in to the granery.

I unpacked, unsadled. and staked
my Mules out, and laid down
under a Mesquit tree. not far from
the house, too smoke and rest. there
was no use of cooking, for I had
nothing to cook. and the worst of all
I had no money to buy any thing

CHAPTER 12

LEAN, LANKY AND HUNGRY

L ittle things makes a fellow feel awful good sometimes. About the most pleased that I ever was in my life was an invitation to dinner once.

In the fall of '77, I was going from the Tombstone country to the Globe district, and as the Indians was very bad, I had kept in the mountains so as to avoid trails and roads, so that they couldn't lay and wait for me. And at the place I speak of is where I came down out of the mountains onto the San Pedro River and from there followed it down to the Gila.

I guess it was about ten o'clock in the morning that I got there and there was a woman herding cows out of the corn and doing her house work too, while her husband, with some Mexicans, was husking and hauling the corn in to the granary. I unpacked, unsaddled and staked my mules out and laid down under a mesquite tree not far from the house to smoke and rest. There was no use of cooking for I had nothing to cook and the worst of all had no money to buy anything with. And I was in hopes that by my being close around when dinner time came, in fact, I calculated to be talking to the man, that he would ask me to have dinner with him. And there was a woman who could cook it so that it would be a real old fashioned country home dinner. The very thoughts of it made my mouth water.

So I watched the sun and that team in the cornfield that they was loading. At last he jumped up on the wagon and in he come and drove up to the granary, where I was as soon as he, and commenced the conversation. And I don't think I ever talked better in my life. It wasn't long till his wife came out and told him dinner was ready, but he kept on talking and, of course, I wouldn't give up my hold on him, especially as he said nothing about grub. His wife seemingly got tired, turned around and went back to the house which was only a very few steps, reminding him that the dinner was getting cold.

At last he started for the house without saying a word to me about dinner. And I sauntered along towards camp, with an extra long face and all the water in my mouth dried up, but I didn't blame him a bit, for I was sure had I told him that I was hungry, or had he suspicioned it, he would have asked me in.

But he hadn't been in the house but a few minutes before he came out and called me in. And I always thought and always shall that his wife sent him back to ask me to come and have some dinner. And I went in and holy Moses, what a dinner, a pot pie, or stew, nice fresh bread, milk and butter. What a spread for a lean, lanky, hungry man like me to set down to, who had been living on venison and who for two years had not sat down to such a table where there was plenty of fresh milk and butter. And didn't it taste good. Wasn't I the happiest man in Arizona, and didn't I eat. And she kept piling it on. I made no apologies for they wasn't necessary. She expected me to eat, and I fully realized her expectations. God bless her. I never saw her afterwards.

In the spring of 82. Old Charlie
O'Farcoit. Jack Young. Young Charlie
Danesbrey. My brother Eff and myself
left San Francisco, on the schooner H2
Sherman, bound for Alaska on a prospec
-ing trip, with a little stern wheel river
steamer on deck, to run up the river's
when we got there, everything went lovely
going out of the bay. And untill we
got out about forty miles. when the
breeze went down leaving us in a dead
Calm, where we remained for three
whole days, then a light storm come
up bring plenty of wind, So that we
done very well the balance of the
way. At Onalaska we put in to
clear the Coustome house, where the
Alaska commercial Company's boys gave
us a dance, of course the girls were
all russian half breeds, or natives, but
they was all good dancers, but what
struck me most was too see those girls
Indian Girls, dressed up, some of
them in silks, and all in the latest
fashions, with pull backs cross hitches
and ruffles, hair banged with kid
gloves on. skin white. & giving every
appearance, of white society ladies

CHAPTER 13

MOUTH OF THE YUKON

In the spring of '82, Old Charlie O. Farcoit, Jack Young, young Charlie Oanesbrey, my brother Eff, and myself left San Francisco on the schooner *H.L. Tiernan*, bound for Alaska on a prospecting trip with a little stern wheel river steamer on deck, to run up the rivers when we got there. Everything went lovely going out of the bay and until we got out about forty miles where the breeze went down leaving us in a dead calm, where we remained for three whole days. Then a light storm come up bringing plenty of wind, so that we done very well the balance of the way. At Onalaska, we put in to clear the custom house, where the Alaska commercial company's boys gave us a dance. Of course, the girls were all Russian half-breeds, or natives, but they was all good dancers. But what struck me most was to see those Indian Girls dressed up, some of them in silks and all in the latest fashions, with full backs, cross hitches and ruffles, hair banged, with kid gloves on, skin white, giving every appearance of white society ladies.

But they could only speak the Russian language and we couldn't, so there wasn't any flirting going on. Still the boys danced if they couldn't talk, and young Charlie told me they was splendid waltzers. A person's impression going in there for the first time is that he is going into an ordinary village of a few hundred inhabitants of white people, for the natives has that appearance until brought face to face with them. Even then, sometimes with a young woman it is a question with you until speaking got her, whether she is not a relation of some of the company's employees or not. But as soon as a favorable breeze came up, which was the second day, we cleared the custom house and steered from St. Michaels, the mouth of the Yukon River, the one we was to ascend and winter on.

As I am a little ahead of my story, I will go back and tell you how I got through the custom house. My steamer being built in San Francisco and over five tons burden. The *New Racket*, as I called her, registering fifteen tons, I had to have a licensed Captain Pilot and engineer. My Engineer was all right for Old Charlie was one and had had his papers for years, not only stationary engines on land but he had served in the Navy as Chief, and all he had to do was to have them renewed. But the Captain and Pilot worried me. Notwithstanding my argument that the boat was altogether a private enterprise and was intended to take the place of a mule, and I would just as soon think of taking out a license for a mule to pack my grub through counties where there was no navigable streams. It, they said, made no difference. It had to go through the same form as if she carried thousands of tons and was made expressly for public use. So the only way out of the difficulty was for me to take out the necessary papers, if I could get them. The boys all said let us once get in the Yukon River, and we will manage her some way between us. And I was the only one that stood a ghost of a

show. So it fell to me. But how was I to pass the
examination. I had never sailed a vessel. Didn't hardly know
which end the rudder was on, and as for my steamboat
experience, it was limited to being a passenger three or four
times on one. Knew nothing about red lights, blue lights, nor
any other kind of lights. But it had to be done, and I got my
papers, but of all the examinations that was ever passed for a
steamboat Captain and Pilot, I guess mine beat them all. For
the only question that I could answer in the affirmative was
for color blindness. That I passed as well as the best. But I
had my papers for Captain Pilot and owner of the *New
Racket* freight and tug steamer built for the Yukon River. It
didn't make a particle of difference. We was all right then. If
we met half a dozen Revenue Cutters and Custom house
officers desiring to see our papers, we had them.

A few days sail from Onalaska brought us to St. Michaels,
about an hour after the *Schooner Leo*, which had left San
Francisco several days after we had bound up to the Arctic
to reline the signal station at Point Barrows, and had on
board a party of miners for Golowin Bay, sixty miles from
St. Michaels on the north side of Norton Sound and not far
from the mouth of Bhering Straits.

We all went ashore, officers and miners from both
vessels, and found at the station Charlie Peterson, whose
station was one hundred and fifty miles up the river, and
Henry Niemann, the agent there, who opened some wine
and beer, which we all seemed to relish. Then we all went on
board the Leo, where Lieut. Powell set out whiskey and more
wine which added to the already merry condition we were
in. Didn't take long to make us extremely jolly and set us to
drinking toasts to everybody we could think of. But it only
lasted a few hours when the Leo was off and we was all at
work unloading and getting ready for our trip up the river.
Having too much stuff for the little boat to carry, I got a

Bidarar from an Indian that would carry about four tons. It
was made of poles, about three inches thick, for timbers and
small sticks, either bent or natural crook for ribs, and all tied
with thongs cut from and covered with Walrus hides.

In a couple of days we were all ready when a storm arose,
which detained us for another day. We were sixty miles from
the mouth of the river, and our boat wouldn't stand much of
a sea, nor would she steer in a high wind, and we had to run
down the coast exposed to the wind and waves. So we had to
watch our chance and improve the first one, for when it
commences storming in that country, it never knows when to
stop. And before it was fairly over, with Charlie Peterson for
Pilot, and the cannons booming that they always fire on the
incoming and outgoing of any vessel, we steamed into the
canal that separates St. Michaels Island from the main land.
Passing through the canal into the Bhering Sea about forty
miles from the mouth of the river and was going along nicely
with Charlie at the wheel. Notwithstanding, there was a stiff
breeze blowing, but Charlie, for years being a seafaring man,
knew how to handle the boat. When Jack Young, thinking it
was about time some of us began to take lessons in steering,
went to the wheel and relieved Charlie after watching him
for a few minutes. And she hadn't went far before he gave
the wheel a turn the wrong way, when she swung around
into the wind and trough of the sea. Nor would she answer
the helm, although Charlie ran to and took the wheel. Still
she headed and seemed determined on going out to sea,
rolling and tumbling waves washing in and over her, looking
as if we were destined to be lost, and for a while it did look
scaly, for she couldn't hold out long the way she was going.
When Charlie told us to get a tent and tie it to the steering
pole and bring one end back towards the pilot house,
making a kind of a jib, which just as soon as was done, she
came around all right, and we ran into the mouth of a small

river that put in there, where we laid for a few hours. Then tried it again.

And got to within about four miles of the mouth of the uphoon, or slough, which was to lead us into the river, the mouth of which was forty or fifty miles still further to the southwest, when we ran aground. It being near low tide where we remained for about ten hours and at one time didn't look much like a sea. For as far as the eye could see, the water only stood in pools, and Indians walked out to us from their village on the land fully five miles away. The Yukon, being a very muddy stream, has formed a bar that they say extends out into the sea sixty miles making it as far as known impossible for sea going vessels to get any closer than St. Michaels. And our little boat only drawing twenty inches of water was laying on the mud high and dry, all of four miles from the nearest point of land. Made it look as if it was a question whether it was going to stay there and wait for another storm to raise the water before we went any farther. As the sun was shining brightly, making it a very pleasant morning barring mosquitoes, but when the time came, the tide came in, and we run into the uphoon and was safe.

The dreaded part of our journey over, for we was practically in the river. The place we all always spoke of as if we can only once get in the river without any mishaps, we can manage the rest, for we had some little idea of what we had to contend with. But as long as we was at sea, we didn't know what might turn up or where we would land, but there we was sure of a landing and if it was too rough would camp. Or if the boat sunk, it wasn't far to swim, and as the banks was on both sides and no chance of heading to sea, I took my first turn at the wheel of a steamboat. And after sending her from one side to the other a few times, nearly running her more into the banks, brought up in the center of the stream, the sweat running down both sides of my backbone and trembling like a leaf. Where I held her, I thought, in good shape, but the boys all said that my course was crookeder than a lamb's tail in fly time. At all events, I managed to keep her in the water until it commenced storming, and the wind raised again. When she got too much for me and Charlie took her, and he didn't run long until he tied up and waited for the wind to lull, which took nearly twenty-four hours. Then we run up, without stopping to Andreasky, Charlie's station. There he stopped, while we went on after laying over a couple of days to dry our skin boats.

I forgot to mention that we had two other fellows along. One an Ethnologist, Jacobson, who came from San Francisco with us, ours being the only vessel coming up at that time, and Wolf, who claimed to be a correspondent for the New York Herald. If he was, I never saw any of his articles, and they had a small *Bidarar* carrying themselves and what few things they had. And when we was in the storm going out to sea, you could have heard Wolf hollow a mile, and afterwards, when asked what he was making so much noise for, he said that he wanted to know where we was going. Something we would have like to have known ourselves about that time.

After leaving Andreasky, went along alright, excepting one or two little mishaps. The first one the second day after wooding up, where there was a strong current and not understanding the art of steering very well. When starting between the wind and current, the boat took a start on me and run down stream. And in making the turn back again, there was a bar close to the shore, and covered with water so as not to be seen, on which I jumped her with a full head of steam on, but fortunately it was mud and sand so that there was no damage done except to detain us for a few hours for we had to partly unload to get her off. The next, a day or two

afterwards, was one of the rudders got loose, the crank pin
came out, but we landed without any trouble. Keyed it up
and made the mission the next day but only stopped to wood
up. The Indians having some wood there for the *Yukon*, the
Alaska Commercial Co.'s steamer, when she should come
down. We bought it with the understanding that they would
get more for the *Yukon*.

Taking another Indian from there to show me the river,
the one I had got from Andreasky claiming not to know the
river any farther, and it being so full of Islands and sloughs
that I was afraid to undertake to hunt my way alone. And
being anxious and in a hurry to get up the river, and to save
time, I got one. Although I had to do all the steering and did
all the way up, which made it pretty hard on me, for we used
to run about eighteen hours a day. The other boys while
running could change off but there was nobody to change
with me.

At Awik, we stopped again a couple of days to dry our
boats and get a new pilot who went with us until we met the
Yukon, where him and Wolf turned back. And where we all
stopped for a few hours for a visit and getting a new pilot
who belonged at Vuliehegt, where we was going to winter.
The next day got to Nulato about noon and where we dried
our boats again. About forty miles above there we ran over
something in the river that knocked one of the rudders off,
loosing the cap to the lower box holding it. But we made a
new one out of wood and went on, losing about an hour's
time. Finally, we rounded a point and there was our station
in sight, and the Indians commenced firing their guns.
Rather a different welcome from what we had been used to
from Indians, and might have frightened us had we not
known that it was a friendly greeting. There we unloaded our
stuff, putting it in one end of the trader's store, it being built
with three rooms to it. Mayo, the trader, kindly gave us one

end of it. And with a *bidarka* that Walker, an opposition trader living twelve miles above, loaned us, I and Eff struck out while the others was building our winter quarters, to see what we could find before housing up for the winter.

The weather then was pleasant. Only an occasional rain and no mosquitoes, but millions of gnats, which bothered some of the boys as bad as the mosquitoes, because they could devise no way of protecting themselves. But we found nothing to attract our notice until the eighth of Oct. when in a gulch, that emptied into a creek about ten miles from the river, we found quite a prospect. Taking a pair of blankets on our backs and killing some pheasants that were very numerous there for something to eat, we camped one night at the gulch. And Eff not being used to such ways, fared pretty hard. He had to set up nearly all night and keep a fire to keep from freezing, for try as he would, he could not roll up and stay so in his blankets. And we didn't have but a pair a piece. Consequently, could not improvise a bed of any kind, and it was very cold which caused him a great deal of suffering. And the next day went to winter quarters, drifting down the river with the anchor ice, but stopped about forty miles down at Walker's, who went down with us the next morning to our winter quarters, but we had to leave our boat on an Island. The slough, between it and where the station being frozen, so that the next day, the eleventh, we went skating.

That night we taxed the keg of whiskey and got a little merry but not drunk because we didn't have it there for that purpose. And when we come to open our supplies for winter use, we found fully half of them damaged, if not more. And some of them so bad that we had to throw them away. Utterly unfit for use, and when I gave the order at Albert Man's and Co. in San Francisco, I told them particular that I want nothing but that what was good and first class articles, for we was going where it was impossible to get anything. And what we didn't have would have to do without, and that was the way they served us. Fortunately we had a large assortment, or we would have fared poorly.

I think it was about the 5th of Nov. that Mayo and myself, with dogs and sleds and an Indian apiece, started for St. Michaels. He going for supplies needed in his trade and I for dogs. Calculating to be back before Christmas, but didn't get back until the 14 of April. When we left the station it was snowing and rather warm, and the snow was soft, so that it was very slow getting along, having to continuously wear snow shoes instead of riding the sled as I had always supposed. For I had so often seen traveling in the arctic regions illustrated as a man setting in a sled wrapped up with furs and the dogs going like the wind. But my experience during that winter was far different. I found out that to ride with dogs and sleds was as necessary to have a good road as anything else, and without it, instead of riding the sled, it would be the snow shoes and walk behind like plowing and steer the sled, there being a pair of handles behind for that purpose.

The first day, we only made about twelve miles, and we had three Indians ahead to break the road. The third one going down the river with us to Novikakit about seventy miles. That night it stormed all night and the next day, so that we laid there, and the next, having no more feed for our dogs and it still storming. And fearing a rain which would make traveling impossible, we returned to Nulukheyt to wait until the weather should settle and get more feed for the dogs, where we stayed until about the 20th, then started again. And all the way to Nulato, which took us about two weeks, the snow was very soft. So much so that it was necessary to break the road to get along at all. And a good deal of the way on the ice under the snow was water, which we would often sink into. Then we would have to stop and clean the ice off from the runners as well as our snowshoes. And which would often occur every few minutes and some it appeared as if we was doing nothing else all day but cleaning our sleds and snow shoes.

But after leaving Nulato, where we stopped to rest a few days, we had a good road for about forty miles down the river to Kaltag, where we left the river, and for the portage across to Norton Sound, about sixty miles where the same slow traveling as we previously experienced was gone over again. Only there was no water and there was several sleds and quite a number of Indians, all on snow shoes, and those that wasn't steering a sled was ahead breaking a road. So that those ˙ behind had a fair road. And when we got to Ulukuk River, twenty-five miles from the Sound, at Ivan's, a Malamute Indian, his wife, was the prettiest woman I think I ever saw. Only she lacked that intelligent look that cultivation gives. But aside from that she was beautiful. A half-breed, her mother being a Malamute woman and her father a Russian, one of the ignorant ones, I suppose a serf. At least he was about the same as an Indian. I noticed wherever I went that the half-breeds were handsome, and some of the children of the traders were pictures.

During our trip across the portage, it was the coldest weather we had during the winter. The morning we left Nulato, the thermometer that Waldron, the trader, had belonging to the signal service, registered 55 degrees below zero, and it seemed to me to be much colder on the portage, a day or two after, than it was that morning, and it would seem almost impossible to camp out and live in such cold weather. But by preparing camp every night, a person can be very comfortable. The mode of preparation is to clear the snow away, making a pit as it were. Then spread some spruce boughs on the ground. Then stick some poles in the banks of snow made by clearing away, always taking care to have the

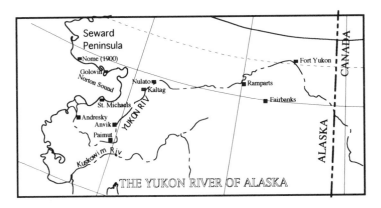

Map of the Yukon River of Alaska

wind right so that the smoke and sparks will pass away. Then around poles, which should stand at about an angle of forty-five degrees, stretch a tarpaulin or sheet of any kind and put some more boughs around the sides so as to break the wind off, should there be any, and build the fire in front, which throws its heat up against the heat and is reflected back, keeping you warm on both sides. And with a few furs to lay on is a very comfortable camp.

Finally, we arrived at St. Michaels a little before Christmas, where I stayed something like a month, having a pleasant time as far as possible under the circumstances. With the two traders, Lawrence and Niemann, and the signal officer, Leavitt, as my companions, as well as Mrs. Lawrence, who done all she could to make my stay as pleasant as possible.

Excerpt from the *San Francisco Chronicle*
BOUND FOR ALASKA
Equipment of a Complete Prospecting Expedition.
Small Stern Wheeler to Navigate the Yukon and Tributaries
Personnel of the Party–The Expedition Outfitted
for Three Years

The prospector who exposes himself to hardship, perils
his life and braves the dangers of the frontier, usually gets more
renown than reward for his services. If he is not rewarded
himself, he has the satisfaction of knowing that he has paved
the way for others and contributed something toward the
progress of civilization and the development of natural resources.
Nothing quickens the enthusiasm of the thoroughbred
prospector sooner than the report that unexplored fields,
reported rich in mineral treasurers are accessible.

An exploring party, headed by Ed. Schieffelin, is about to
leave San Francisco to visit a country that has never been
prospected by Americans, and as far as historical records
indicate, never even seen by white men. It is calculated that
the prospectors will be absent three years, and make ... many
thousands of miles by sea ... In the outset a brief photograph of
the leader may be acceptable. He is known in the southwest
as a progressive, dauntless and successful prospector. He came
from Pennsylvania to the Pacific Coast as a child in 1856, and
subsequently located mines in Nevada, Utah, Arizona and
California. He estimates that he has located one thousand claims.

PROSPECTING NEAR COCHISE'S STRONGHOLD

In 1877 he visited what is now the famous Tombstone
District of Arizona. Alone and depending solely on his rifle
for food, he lived in that region for months. Indians hostile
to white men and particularly hostile to explorers held sway
in the rugged mountains of Arizona. They saw him not, and
neither did he see the redskins. Yet the headquarters of
Chief Cochise (then living) was within nine miles of the

prospector's camp. As Schieffelin expresses it, "you don't see a hostile Indian until you hear from him. When you see him, it is too late."

EXPERIENCES IN THE TOMBSTONE DISTRICT.

The prospector, modestly referring to his life on the frontier, said in a recent interview at the office of Albert Man & Co., that he went into Tombstone with $40, and he and his brother "Eff" * each went out of camp with $600,000. He located the famous Contention mine in 1878, and afterwards sold it for $20,000. It has since made many men rich. He discovered also the "Toughnut," "Goodenough" and "Lucky Cuss."

PREPARING FOR NEW FIELDS.

Ed. Schieffelin is looking for a new field. Civilization is encroaching upon Arizona, and the man whose best days have been passed on the frontier has listened for years to the reports of ... mineral wealth in Alaska. The breadth and ruggedness of the country challenged the prospector. It inspired him to the highest ambition of the explorer, and having the pecuniary resources at hand to outfit an expedition and finding nervy and stalwart young men, full of enthusiasm, and energy, ready to cast their fortunes with his own, they decided to see the lands and waters of Alaska. A few weeks ago he came to San Francisco and charted a schooner to take him to St. Michaels. In the first place he decided to build a small steamboat to navigate the Yukon River and tributary streams. The boat is a stern wheeler, fifty-three feet long and drawing fifteen inches of water, and is capable of carrying forty tons of freight and the exploring party. The craft, which has been christened the "*New Racket*," is equipped with two engines, 8-inch cylinder and 24-inch stroke. The steamer will be hoisted aboard the schooner, and launched at a point where the Yukon empties into the ocean. The machinery was constructed by the Main-street Iron Works in this city.

PERSONNEL OF THE PARTY.

A few words concerning the personnel of the expedition may not come amiss. Ed. Schieffelin is chief, and his subordinates or companies are Eff Schieffelin, Charles Farcoit (Engineer), Charles Sauerberry and Jack Young. Every man in the party has been tried and tested in physical strength, nerve, frontier skill and general staying qualities. Young is suffering from a bullet wound in the leg, which he received in an encounter in Arizona with cowboys, having been called to assist the officers of the law in arresting desperadoes. The leader is the smallest man in the party, yet he is five feet seven inches high and weighs 180 pounds, with hardly an ounce of superfluous flesh. He may be recognized on the streets of San Francisco by his ample growth of dark hair, his frontier bearing and border costume. There is not a drinking man in the expedition. In fact, the entire supply of liquor for the three years' campaign consists of ten gallons of whisky and five gallons of brandy, and yet the party of five take along 7,000 pounds of flour and 500 pounds of coffee.

*... OF THE YUKON.

... condition is perfect. In se-... Schieffelin had the advantage of *... Simpson's experience, that gentleman having ascended the Yukon River for a distance of 1,500 miles and gained many points concerning the resources of the country. He describes the river as carrying a volume of water apparently equal to the Mississippi, and says the scenery is impressive and picturesque beyond description. The Tananna River empties into the Yukon about 1,500 miles from the sea, and is said to be navigable for 1,000 miles or more. Above the confluence of these rivers the Yukon is navigable for 1,200 miles. The streams are full of fine salmon and the country abounds with moose and reindeer.

PROGRAMME OF EXPEDITION–EQUIPMENT.

It is the intention of the explorers to get a pilot at St. Nicholas about the middle of July, and immediately ascend the Yukon to the mouth of the Tananna, where a supply base will be established. Aside from provisions of all necessary kinds for three years, the expedition is supplied with picks, shovels, axes, mining tools, assaying apparatus, giant powder cartridges, heavy woolen clothing, camp equipage, such as cooking utensils, and last, but not least, a Sharp's rifle and two revolvers for each man, and a fully supply of fixed ammunition of the best quality.

One shotgun is to be taken along to kill ducks, geese and small birds. Schieffelin relies mainly on the rifle for purposes of protection and hunting. He is particularly partial to the Sharp rifle, having reached the conviction that it is the best mountain gun yet invented. His own rifle was made to order. It is an eighteen-pound gun, caliber 54, and cost $160. Trouble with the natives is not expected, but in case any difficulty should occur the prospectors want to be fixed so they can take care of themselves. Schieffelin says the story of the stranger in Texas is applicable to Alaska. The stranger in Texas was advised that a revolver was not often required, but when it was needed, it was needed "awful bad."

The steamer will wood up along the banks of the streams, and tie up for the nights. As the Alaska days are about twenty hours long in summer, the boys expect to put in full time. Where good prospects are discovered cribs will be constructed to keep out the snow, and the work of sinking the shaft prosecuted during the winter months.

The prospectors will look mainly for quartz, but calculate on keeping an eye out for all valuable minerals. Schieffelin's reason for supposing that Alaska is rich in mineral treasures is founded on the theory that it is within the direct mineral belt which extends from Cape Horn through South America,

Mexico, the United States and British Columbia, as far north as prospectors have gone, and then skipping Alaska (unexplored) is disclosed again in Siberia. He says: "This, I think, is the mineral belt which encircles the world, and the proof is strong enough to take chances."

PREPARATIONS FOR WINTER.

In the course of the interview yesterday, Ed. Schieffelin said the party was prepared to winter wherever winter should overtake the expedition. It is calculated to use Eskimo dogs and sledges for inland expeditions during the winter months. It is possible that a boat of the Alaska Fur Company may establish communication with the prospectors within the next three years, but the leader of the party does not rely on outside assistance. The outfit of supplies, costing not less than $20,000 was purchased in this city during the past few days. "I count three years," said Schieffelin, "from this fall. We just make a start this year; that's why I throw this year in. We expect to get into winter quarters this fall, right in the heart of the country. I feel at home right out in the mountains, where there are just a few men. I don't feel at home in this city; rather be on the frontier than anywhere else."

Schieffelin brightened up when the enthusiasm of the little prospecting party was mentioned. He said the boys were full of it—anxious to go to an unknown region, where no prospector had ever been.

If rich mines are discovered, the leader of the party will return to San Francisco and order mining machinery purposely for the handling of quartz in that region.

*Page torn—unable to read

*Editor's Note: Should be his brother Al.

San Francisco Chronicle, July 14, 1884
DOWN THE YUKON RIVER
Traveling Twelve Hundred Miles in Search of Gold.

A *CHRONICLE* reporter called the other day upon "Ed" Schieffelin, who last year made a trip of some 1,200 miles down the Yukon river for the purpose of prospecting for gold. Mr. Schieffelin has been a prospector from his earliest youth, first starting out in this business at the age of 14 in Oregon and for the last fifteen years he has explored this entire western coast from Alaska to Mexico.

"We hired the *H.L. Tiernan*," he said. " She was a schooner of 125 to 150 tons burden, and we left this port on June 13, 1883, and arrived at St. Michael's on July 25th. On August 3d we got into the mouth of the Yukon river. The scenery is of a most uninteresting description. On the north and west is a low range of hills, and on the south and east sides is a vast swampy country, covered with underbrush and moss. Where it empties into the Behring sea the river is broad, having several mouths. At present the principal of these separate streams has not been found, and consequently it is extremely difficult to enter the river. But there is no doubt that there is a main mouth. My reasons for so thinking are that the known channels are too narrow to permit of the passage of the ice-packs and driftwood into the ocean. For 1,000 miles this river is broad, full of sloughs, islands and bars; it then strikes a range of hills called the Ramparts. The character of the river then changes, and for 150 miles it is deep, with a strong current, and is from three-fourths of a mile to a mile broad. Then it opens out again into a vast plain, or *tundra*, which lies above Fort Yukon, in British Possessions. Then again it enters mountainous regions and branches out into various streams."

"Do you think this river is navigable?"

Edward Lawrence Schieffelin

"Of course it is. It is navigable for at least 1,000 to 1,800 miles. But the country will never amount to anything. The climate will not permit of it. The surface of the land is as completely covered with moss as is this floor with carpet. The

heat of the sun can never penetrate this mossy covering and
it is only a few places where the land is so exposed as to
permit of the sun's ray lighting on if for any length of time.
Then the country is so densely covered with a growth of
scrub and brushwood that if effectually prevents the ground
from thawing and I believe the land is frozen eternally."

"Is there anything to be realized from this country?"

"We can only expect fish and fur. The fish are splendid,
the king salmon being especially fine. It beats any salmon
that I have ever eaten, even the Columbia river salmon or
anything along the coast. It may eventually become a mining
country, but that will be when the rest of our mining country
is exhausted and our miners have nowhere else to go.
The difficulties encountered on such an expedition are
extraordinary. There are no animals there and what is more,
there is no way of keeping them. A man has to pack his own
supplies directly he leaves his canoe. Besides, he has to
provide himself with a hatchet, with which he has to cut his
way through the brush. He can avoid this by taking to the
tops of the mountains and following the moose trails. And
then in the summer it is worse, for it rains so much during
this season that a man cannot keep himself dry."

"Are there good indications of gold?"

"Oh, yes; you can find gold almost anywhere. But the
only heavy gold that was found in the country up to the time
we were there was discovered by us in the gulches of the
mountains known as the Ramparts. But fine scale gold can
be found on almost any of the bars in small quantities. In
the Ramparts $15 a day can probably be secured, whilst on
the bars scale gold amounting to $3 or $4 per day."

"Your idea of going up there was for prospecting?"

"Certainly, that was the object of our trip. We were five
in the party and we prospected from 1,000 to 1,200 miles
along the Yukon river."

"Did you experience many hardships?"

"We had plenty of hard work cutting and wading through the river, and carrying our hatchet and our supplies is no joke. I can assure you. And then mind you we were all Arizona men. We had come straight from that hot country, and most of us had malaria in our systems. One would have thought that we would not have been able to stand the change from the intense heat to the extreme cold. But we did. There was not a cough or cold in our whole party. We all came back stronger—with the exception of one who stayed up there. We were in the country eighteen months."

"Have you any idea of going up there again?"

"No, sir; nor would I advise anybody to go there—not for any purpose—unless he wanted to die of starvation."

"What do you think of Lieutenant Stoney's expedition?"

"He claims to have discovered a river which empties itself into Kotzehue sound. I can hardly see how he can lay claim to such a discovery, as the presence of this river was certainly known to the white men resident up there. Nor can it be a very large stream; perhaps it is as big as the Sacramento river. I will give you the reasons for my thinking it cannot be a very large stream: First, because the Keokuk river is one which heads in that same country and empties into the Yukon some 800 miles from its mouth, as does also the Colville river, which runs into the Arctic. Now, both of these rivers rise in the country which lies between the Yukon and the Arctic ocean and which certainly has not sufficient expanse to support any very large river."

"Are there any white men in that section of the country now?"

"There are. No less than twelve men wintered there this year. They are all prospecting. I think our action may have induced these men to make the attempt, for they are all Arizona men. They made sure we would strike something and thought they would like to be in with us. They went first to Harrisburg, and then crossed over the mountains, struck the headwaters of the Yukon, built there their boats and then came down stream to the place where we made our richest discoveries."

"Do you think they will stay there long?"

"No; I do not. I think that most of them will come down by the *St. Paul* and I am pretty sure they will be disgusted with their venture."

Just about as thin a dress as I
ever saw, was on some Indians
at a village in Alaska called
Paimute.

In the winter of 82 & 83.
I was in that country and traveled a large part of it with
dogs and sled, and some time
was in company of some of
the traders. that was living at
diferent stations trading in
furs, among the Indians,

At this time of which I am
speaking, I and Ned Lind left
St Michaels. on Norton Sound
for Kolmankofsky. an station
on the Kuskukuim river
about three hundred miles
in an easterly direction
We went across the country.
from St Michaels. too and
down the Anvik river. too
the Anvik station, at the mouth
and where the Anvik empties
into the Yukon. about one hundred
and fifty miles, then down
the Yukon. about fifty miles
to Paimute. then across the

CHAPTER 14

THE LIGHTEST EVENING DRESS

Just about as thin a dress as I ever saw was on some Indians at a village in Alaska called Paimute.

In the winter of '82 and '83, I was in that country and traveled a large part of it with dogs and sled and sometimes was in company of some of the traders that was living at different stations trading in furs among the Indians.

At this time of which I am speaking, I and Ned Lind left St. Michaels on Norton Sound for Kolmankofsky, a station on the Kuskus Kurin River about three hundred miles in an easterly direction. We went across the country from St. Michaels to and down the Anvik River to the Anvik Station at the mouth, and where the Anvik empties into the Yukon, about one hundred and fifty miles. Then down the Yukon

119

about fifty miles to Paimute. Then across the country to about one hundred miles to Kolmankofsky.

The night we stopped at Paimute, the Indians were having an *Eqruska*, or dance and there was quite a number from other villages there, together with those belonging there. It being a village of probably fifteen hundred, made quite a crowd, so that their *Cazhim* was as full as it would hold conveniently. Still they made room for us in one corner, it being the place where they always take strangers.

It is built partially underground like all their winter habitations anywhere near the coast. And is entered by a tunnel and hole cut in the center of the floor, which is composed of spruce boards split and hewed out. A portion in the center around the hole is loose so as to be removed when necessary to build a fire to heat it up, which is about once a week. The smoke escaping through a hole in the center of the roof, which is afterwards covered with a transparent covering made of seal gut, the only means of light during the day. At night using seal oil, which is held in a store basin nearly as large as an ordinary wash bowl using for a wick, moss, and standing on a post about three feet from the floor. It can be imagined what it must be when lit. That rancid oil and green moss burning together sending up a stream of black smoke and, where there is two or three of them burning at once, and the room full of Indians of all sexes and ages without the least ventilation, and that for hours at a time, what it must be like. The inside on an average is thirty or forty feet square. The walls built out of poles about ten feet long split in half and set on end. The cracks chucked with moss, the roof having four sides to it and coming to a center where the hole is for the smoke to go out. The whole thing underground. The dirt used in excavating for to put the house in, is put on the roof, a little house over the door at the entrance of the tunnel to keep the snow from piling upon it and a plank about two feet wide around the inside of the house about three feet from the floor. I believe completes the description of what a *Cazhim* or *Barabara* is. For they are both built alike. One is for a hall or whatever you are a mind to call it. It is where all councils and dances or anything of that description is held. While the other is for habitation, or a house, where different families live.

When we arrived, they were not dancing but that evening they asked Ned if we had any objections to their continuing their dance, and he asked me. I told him no, to let them go ahead. So at it they went, and after three or four hours, they concluded to have supper. Or at least I supposed it was supper. At all events the women brought in *Kantags* (a dish of all sizes made out of birch, a hoop something like a cheese hoop with a bottom to it) full of all kinds of stinking stuff and placed them on the floor in front of some old men that I had noticed lounging on the plank and thought they were naked. And they were as far as my judgment on such things goes. But after the women had brought in all they intended to and all was seated, girls and boys, men and women, old and young, three of these old fellows that was naked got up and commenced handing the eatables around. Doing the honors as it were and coming to us, offered or asked if we would have anything. I declined, Ned took something. I have forgotten what.

Then I saw what I thought my eyes had deceived me in, and that he had drawn the foreskin over the head of his penis and tied a string around it. The only semblance of clothing, if that might be called, such that he had on. I asked Ned what the devil was that string there for. "Why," he says, "they don't consider they are naked when that is on. Don't you see, it hides the head of it. And that according to their custom is what they call naked. When one of those others over there that is naked gets up, if he hasn't got the string on, he will cover it with his hand or something." Which was true. For a few minutes before I had noticed one of them walking across the floor and holding his hand over it. And that with the indifference in which those other three was walking around, together with Ned being well acquainted with their habits, having, until a year or two previously, lived within a few miles of that village for a few years, and was conversant with their habits. At least that was his explanation, and from what I saw I believe it.

It is a little, the lightest evening dress that I ever saw. A piece of string about the size of an ordinary shoe string and about a foot long. But it shows what custom does. There wasn't a soul paying any attention to them but me, anymore than if they had all the clothes they could carry on them.

It was in the spring of 83. that I saw
what I am telling you. At a place called
Nulato, about six hundred miles up the
Yukon river. in Alaska.

In Alaska. the dogs go mad, or have
fits, which in that country they call mad
-ness. at all events they have all the sym
-toms of hydrophobia, except that they don't
seem to attempt to bite a person, but
snap and bite at anything else that
comes in their way, And everything that
they bite, has the same disease, whether
it is hydrophobia or what not.

It was while traveling with dogs, and
on my way home, after being gone all
winter, I stopped there a couple of days
to rest, as I had something like three
hundred miles farther to go, The night
before I started one of the Indian's dogs
went mad, And as usual. the Indians
under took to kill it with Clubs, And
after about ten minutes of quite an
exciting time, and too their appearance
a good deal of sport, they succeeded, or
supposed they had, And to all appeare
-nces, the dog was dead, he lay stretch
out just under the bank of the river, and
close to the road that I was too take

CHAPTER 15

MAD DOGS

It was in the spring of '83 that I saw what I am telling you. At a place called Nulato, about six hundred miles up the Yukon River in Alaska.

In Alaska, the dogs go mad or have fits, which in that country they call madness. At all events, they have all the symptoms of hydrophobia, except that they don't seem to bite a person, but snap and bite at anything else that comes in their way. And everything that they bite has the same disease, whether it is hydrophobia or what not.

It was while traveling with dogs and on my way home after being gone all winter, I stopped there a couple of days to rest, as I had something like three hundred miles farther to go. The night before I started, one of the Indian's dogs went mad and as usual, the Indians undertook to kill it with clubs. And after about ten minutes of quite an exciting time and to them apparently a good deal of sport, they succeeded or supposed they had. And to all appearances the dog was dead. He lay stretched out just under the bank of the river and close to the road that I was to take in the morning, the blood running out of his nose, stiff as a post.

In the morning when I started on, passing where he laid, I noticed that he was curled up and breathing and looked like a dog asleep, but I went on not stopping to examine him or give him any farther thought than that he must be tough to stand such a beating and live. For it was the intentions of the Indians to kill him and seemed to try hard enough, for when they succeeded in knocking him down after several very hard licks, mostly in the neighborhood of his head, they then struck him three or four times on his forehead hard enough I thought to kill most anything, causing him to stiffen and tremble like any animal that is killed by having their skull crushed.

The following fall, when I left the country for San Francisco, the trader, Capt. Waldren, who was at Nulato at the time, was there at St. Michaels, the port for that country where I was a few days before the Revenue Cutter arrived that brought me to San Francisco. And we incidentally got a talking about the circumstances, when he told me that that dog got well and was alive and hearty as any dog in the country. And that that was not the only case where they had got well under similar treatment, that he himself knew of quite a number of cases. And he said that it was usually conceded by the Indians that if they lived, although they tried to kill them, they go well. The White men usually shoot them, not only to relieve them of their suffering, which seems to be intense, but to protect them from the cruelty of the Indians.

I had two that went mad. One I didn't see, the other was where I was at a station during the winter, and was a dog that I had but a day or two previous bought from an Indian. And I being a stranger to him, had him chained to keep him from running away. And I never saw anything like him. His eyes was green and the slime running from his mouth, white and of a frothy substance, but the nearest comparison I can make is the white of an egg. It resembled that more than anything else and a profusion of it. Although it was middle winter and very cold, he seemed to be in a very high fever. And constantly struggled with all his might to break loose, and paid but little attention to anybody around him and acted as though he was in the most intense agony standing on his hind feet, howl, yelp and snap continually. But no barking, and as soon as I saw him, I had him shot.

What effect the beating given by the Indians has on them, I don't know. Consequently offer no suggestions, but would like some scientist try and see if he could offer any. For instance, what would Pasteur think of such a treatment for hydrophobia.

Destination Tombstone

NOTES

Silver From Spanish Missions to Space Age Missiles, by Charles
   H. Dunning with Edward H. Peplow, Jr. Hicks
   Publishing Corp., Pasadena, California, 1966

1. Brunckow Mine discovered by Frederick Brunckow in
   1857. Brunckow was later murdered by Mexican helpers.
   Mine located five miles west of the later Tombstone,
   three or four miles east of Charleston.
2. McCracken Mine located 165 miles west of Tombstone;
   lies east of Yucca in Mohave County; a few miles
   southwest of Wickieup on highway 93 at Signal. Was
   discovered in 1874.
3. Governor A.P.K. Safford visited Tombstone mines in
   1879 and made a deal to build a ten-stamp mill for a
   quarter interest in the Toughnut claim.
4. In 1880 Southern Pacific Railroad had reached Tucson
   from the west. By late 1880 reached San Pedro River
   where Benson was established. In 1884, the Santa Fe
   constructed a line from Benson to Fairbanks, Nogales
   and Guaymas. It was later bought by the Southern Pacific.

History of Arizona and New Mexico, 1530-1888, by Hubert
  Howe Bancroft, Horn & Wallace Publishers,
  Albuquerque, New Mexico, 1962.

5. Tombstone Mines were the most productive of all,
  having yielded about $30,000,000. The most famous
  mines or companies were the Contention, Grand Central
  and Tombstone which were a depth of 750 feet.
  Extensive pumping machinery was completed in 1883 for
  working the water level.

Rock to Riches, by Charles H. Dunning; Southwest Publishing
  Company, Inc.; Phoenix, Arizona

6. Contention Mine was named because of a dispute on
  ownership between prospectors Oliver Bayer and Henry
  Williams.
7. Governor Safford organized the Tombstone Mill and
  Mining Company.
8. In 1880 the Schieffelin interest in the Tombstone Mill
  and Mining Co. and the Corbin Mill and Mining Co. was
  purchased for $600,000 by a syndicate of Eastern Capitalists.
  Gird retained his interest and for about a year was manager.
  When he later sold his interest for more than the
  Schieffelins had received for theirs, he divided with them.

Roadside History of Arizona, by Marshall Trimble; Mountain
  Press Publishing Company, Missula, 1986

9. On March 8, 1877 a temporary military post was located
  at the foot of the Huachucha Mountains partially to keep
  Apaches out of Mexico. In 1882, a resurgence of Apache
  warfare caused Fort Huachucha to be upgraded to a
  permanent military post.
10. In traveling from the McCracken Mine to Tombstone,
  Ed Schieffelin went southeast to Phoenix, crossed the Salt
  River at Hayden's Ferry, then south to Tucson; then to
  the San Pedro Valley, south at St. David and followed the
  San Pedro River up stream to Narrows.

INDEX

ORDER FORM

☐ Yes! Please send me the titles I've selected below.

Name_____

Address_____

City_____ State_____ Zip_____

Phone_____ Fax_____

Title	Qty.	Each	Total
Destination Tombstone, Adventures of a Prospector Edward Schieffelin, Founder of Tombstone	_____	$14.95	_____
Tombstone, A 60 Minute Audio Magazine (audio cassette) narrated by Timothy R. Walters True tales from the "town too tough to die," w/ map. Hear the stories of Tombstone, one of the most colorful towns in the Old West.	_____	$12.00	_____
SAVE! Combination book and audio tape	_____	$25.00	_____
	Subtotal		_____
Arizona residents include 7% sales tax.	Tax		_____
	S&H		$ 3.00
	TOTAL		_____

Please add $3.00 per order shipping & handling. Foreign orders must be accompanied by a postal money order in U.S. funds.

Send check or money order to:
Royal Spectrum Publishing
2562 E. Evergreen, Mesa, Arizona 85213

To order by phone call 1 (800) 484-2271, code 6419.
In Arizona, call (602) 969-1591 or fax (602) 969-1730.
Contact Royal Spectrum Publishing about quantity discounts.

About The Author

Marilyn Butler, a native of California, lives in Gilbert, Arizona, with her husband, Glen. She is retired and has two children, three step-children and one granddaughter. She volunteers at the local library and enjoys painting, needlework, hiking and golf.